DEVON
GHOSTS & LEGENDS

Hannah

moneanana

is the

best

2468 WHO DO we

a$ presheate Not

the king Not tue queen

but Hannah montanana

DEVON
GHOSTS & LEGENDS

MIKE HOLGATE

HALSGROVE

First published in Great Britain by Halsgrove, 2009

British Library Cataloguing-in-Publication Data
A CIP record for this title is available from the British Library

ISBN 978 1 84114 951 6

HALSGROVE
Halsgrove House,
Ryelands Industrial Estate,
Bagley Road, Wellington, Somerset TA21 9PZ
Tel: 01823 653777 Fax: 01823 216796
email: sales@halsgrove.com

Part of the Halsgrove group of companies
Information on all Halsgrove titles is
available at: www.halsgrove.com

Printed and bound by
Short Run Press, Exeter

CONTENTS

ACKNOWLEDGEMENTS

The author would like to express his gratitude for access to illustrations, books, newspapers and on-line resources available at the John Pike Local Studies Room, Torbay Library Services.

The famous White Lady Waterfall, Lydford.

INTRODUCTION

Holiday Haunts and Kindred Spirits

It is an incredible phenomenon that among the anonymous grey monks, white ladies, limping nuns and headless horsemen that haunt the county of Devon, there have been reported sightings of a host of highly recognisable celebrity ghosts.

These include royal figures Richard the Lionheart, Lady Jane Grey and the Duke of Monmouth; high ranking churchmen Saint Thomas Beckett and Bishop Henry Phillpotts; Elizabethan seadogs Walter Raleigh, Humphrey Gilbert and Francis Drake; writers Oscar Wilde, Charles Kingsley and Beatrice Chase; famous personalities: Lady Nancy Astor, Lillie Langtry, Isadora Duncan, Isambard Kingdom Brunel and Lawrence of Arabia. Spooky goings-on in our holiday haunts often involve kindred spirits – ghosts who haunt in pairs or groups – such as the Duke of Somerset and Lady Jane Seymour and the legendary Uncle Tom Cobley and all.

In addition, writers Rudyard Kipling, Beverley Nichols and Violet Tweedale have related their personal experiences of haunted houses, while ghost hunters with rich imaginations have interpreted the sound of footsteps to be those of either Charles I or William of Orange and the apparition of a black pig

Berry Pomeroy – Devon's most haunted castle where more than two dozen ghosts have been spotted including the Duke of Somerset and Lady Jane Seymour.

to be the transformed soul of Richard Grenville or Judge Jeffries.

The fascinating stories of these famous lives and supernatural tales of their restless spirits in the afterlife have been compiled in a veritable who's who of phantoms that roam Devon – surely the ghost capital of this haunted isle – for, it is a curious fact that every year there are more reported sightings of supernatural activity in Britain than the combined total recorded by the rest of the world.

Mike Holgate
Torquay, November 2008

King Arthur meets the Lady of the Lake.

KING ARTHUR

The Lady of Slapton Ley

Legends flourish throughout the West Country about the exploits of the great King Arthur (c500AD). However, Devon's Arthurian tales have been largely overshadowed by the competing claims of her neighbouring counties. Cornwall's case is based on the theories that Arthur was born at Tintagel Castle and the site of the royal court of Camelot was Killibury Hill Fort near Wadebridge. Accordingly, the scene of Arthur's fatal Battle of Camlan was fought at Slaughter Bridge on the River Camel and the Lady of the Lake rose from Dozmary Pool on Bodmin Moor to reclaim the king's sword Excalibur. Somerset's version of events would have us believe that Camelot was based at Cadbury Castle, near Wincanton and that Arthur's death occurred at the hands of the evil Mordred on the banks of the River Cam. Furthermore, his body lies buried alongside Queen Guinevere at Glastonbury Abbey where medieval monks unearthed a red cross inscribed: 'Here lies the renowned King Arthur and Guinevere his wife in the isle of Avalon'.

Half-man, half-myth, the search for the 'real' Arthur has led many historians to reach the conclusion that he was a chieftain of the Ancient Britons, ruling an area from Cornwall to the Mendips during the Dark Ages. Following the departure of the Romans, he fought in the interests of the national cause against the invasion of the Saxons. Medieval writers created the romantic notion of the noble Knights of the Round Table and their Quest for the Holy Grail. The prime source of these legends was Geoffrey of Monmouth's Twelfth Century account compiled in a *History of the Kings of Great Britain* which began with the mythical founding of Britain by the exiled Trojan prince Brutus who stepped ashore in Devon and according to the words of an old local rhyme declared: 'Here I sit and here I rest, this place shall be called Totnes'.

It is a curious fact that only the Devil has given his name to more British landmarks than King Arthur and both are featured prominently in the landscape of Dartmoor. The legendary Arthur was raised by the wizard Merlin, whose magical powers were granted as the result of him being the offspring of a nun and an incubus – a demon believed in folklore to have been sent from Hell to impregnate

The Lady of the Lake comforts the ailing knight.

sleeping women and undo the good work of Jesus Christ. This was part of the Devil's grand design to capture souls and perpetuate evil, a plan that could easily be thwarted by ensuring that all babies were baptised in the name of God. Arthur was denied such protection by the church when they learned he had been conceived by a wicked act of deception. In return for a promise that he could claim any resultant child, Merlin cast a spell on the besotted King Uther so that he resembled Gorlois, the Duke of Cornwall, which allowed him to seduce the duke's wife Igraine. She believed she was making love to her husband and therefore, unwittingly committed adultery and fell pregnant by Uther. King Uther then ruthlessly arranged for Gorlois to be sent to the front line and killed in battle, clearing the way to marry his widow, but when their son Arthur was born, the church refused to baptise the child of this illicit union.

Merlin enabled Arthur to draw the sword from the stone that established his right to become the true king of England. Arthur then created the order of the Round Table to fight for the cause of justice and ignored Merlin's warning that his bravest knight Sir Lancelot would have an affair with his wife Queen Guinevere, which would lead to the destruction of the realm and Arthur's death. However, the wizard was powerless to foresee his own downfall when he became infatuated with the Lady of the Lake, who according to the people of the South Hams rises from the waters of Slapton Ley. Using her feminine wiles, she tricked the unsuspecting Merlin into teaching her his magical secrets that she then used to imprison him in a cave. The spell that holds him there can only be broken when Arthur rules again, a story that underpins the popular belief that whenever Britain is endangered, the great man is reincarnated at the country's hour of need. This line of heroes includes Devon seadog Sir Francis Drake who masterminded the defeat of the Spanish Armada.

King Arthur's son Sir Mordred was born as a result of an incestuous relationship with his sister Morgause, although he was totally unaware that they were related. Father and son became rivals for the kingdom and slew each other in battle. In Devon legend, the mortally wounded Arthur instructed Sir Bedivere to take his enchanted sword Excalibur and throw it into a nearby stretch of water at Slapton Ley where it was caught by the hand of the Lady of the Lake. As King Arthur's body was transported to the mystical isle of Avalon, located at Burgh Island off the coast of Bigbury-on-Sea, Dewer the Devil reclaimed his soul and condemned his spirit to lead the dreaded Wisht Hunt, a spectral pack of hounds who are themselves the transformed souls of un-baptised children – the very quarry they pursue across Dartmoor. To escape responsibility for this onerous task, King Arthur challenged the Evil One's authority. Climbing to the top of Hel Tor, near Mortenhamstead, he spotted Dewer standing on Blackingstone and hurled quoits at him. As he was driven off, Dewer flew into a terrible rage and transformed the missiles into giant stone rings, which still encircle each tor and are known as Arthur's Quoits.

SAINT THOMAS BECKET

The Sword of Bovey Tracey

On Christmas Day 1170, the long standing feud between Henry II and the Archbishop of Canterbury, Thomas Becket (c1118-1170), finally erupted when news reached the king at court in France that Becket, recently reinstated after spending six years in exile, had excommunicated the bishops who had officiated at Henry's coronation during his absence and according to them was ready to 'tear the crown from the young king's head'. The monarch was enraged, 'What a pack of fools and cowards have I nourished in my household' he cried, 'that not one of them will avenge me of this turbulent priest'.

William de Tracy, Reginald fitzUrse, Hugh de Murville, and Richard le Breton were stung into action by this outburst and immediately set sail for England believing they had the king's blessing. The four knights rode to Canterbury and when they entered the archbishop's chamber, Sir William de Tracy was the only one whom Thomas recognised and greeted by name. A ferocious argument ensued and the knights left to arm themselves and returned to the cathedral an hour later to carry out their vow to slay Becket. Tracy strode forward and warned,

'Flee! Thou art death's man', but was seized by the archbishop who flung him aside. Several sword blows then rained down on the defenceless churchman and Tracy struck the fatal blow that sliced off the crown of his head causing his brains to spill out onto the floor.

Becket's death sealed the self-fulfilling prophesy he had made when first offered the post by his former friend Henry: 'Should God permit me to be Archbishop I should lose your majesty's favour'. Their quarrels had stemmed from the issue of whether the State or Church should have jurisdiction in ecclesiastical matters, particularly in the case of a lawbreaking cleric's right to be tried in church courts. The murder provoked great indignation across Europe and miracles reportedly occurred to pilgrims visiting Becket's tomb. In 1173, the pope canonised Thomas and King Henry was forced to visit Canterbury to pay penance and was ceremoniously whipped by monks as he left the abbey. Immediately after the murder, William de Tracy returned to his own diocese and made a confession to Bishop Bartholomew of Exeter, then surrendered himself to the pope's mercy. He and his fellow conspirators were ordered to spend fourteen years with the Templars and adhere to a lifelong penance of fasting and prayer. Tracy set out for the Holy Land in 1173, but got no further than Cosenza in Sicily. There he contracted a terrible wasting disease and died in agony, tearing away the decaying flesh from his body whilst praying incessantly for forgiveness from St Thomas. On his deathbed he made out a charter granting his Devon manor of Doccombe to the chapter of Canterbury 'for the love of God,

The assassination of Thomas Beckett at Canterbury Cathedral.

the salvation of my own soul and my ancestors' souls, and for the love of the blessed Thomas, archbishop and martyr, of venerable memory'.

The de Tracy family hailed from the Norman village of Traci near Bayeaux. The family seat in Devon was located at Morthoe and it seems probable that Henry de Tracy was granted the Barony of Barnstaple during the reign of Henry II's predecessor, King Stephen. William de Tracy's pedigree is uncertain but there is a compelling theory that his grandfather was sired by Henry I who publicly acknowledged only twenty of his numerous illegitimate offspring. Therefore, this branch of the de Tracy family took the mother's name and held the Baronies of Woollacombe and Bradninch. Following the murder of Thomas Becket, all members of the de Tracy family felt shamed and undertook charitable work in the county to atone for the wrongdoing.

Despite the fact that there is no evidence that Thomas Becket ever visited Devon, there is an intriguing myth associated with William de Tracy's motives for taking part in the assassination. The tale relates how the archbishop visited Buckfast Abbey and later journeyed to Bovey Tracey where he was entertained by de Tracy and his wife. Later, while her husband was attending King Henry's court in France, Lady de Tracy invited the churchman to counsel her on religious matters, but this was misconstrued by Sir William who believed these liaisons were evidence of an affair. After the grim deed, Sir William retreated to Morthoe and sent for his wife who was horrified to learn of her husband's misguided jealousy. The shock of Becket's death caused her to go into premature labour and the couple's son was stillborn. Filled with remorse for doubting the integrity of Lady de Tracy and Sir Thomas, William decided to erect churches dedicated to the memory of the saint at Morthoe, Bovey Tracy and Barnstaple.

According to legend, William de Tracy broke his sword as a gesture of remorse and threw it into the river. The pieces were found and welded together and put on display at The Riverside Hotel in Bovey Tracey. Devonians have another constant reminder of William de Tracy's treachery, for, the ghost of St Thomas Becket gallops through the village of Lapford on his way to Nymet Tracey at midnight on each anniversary of his death.

RICHARD I
& QUEEN BERENGARIA

The Lionheart of Buckfast Abbey

In 1981, Father Abbot Leo Smith of Buckfast Abbey recounted to the *Totnes Times*, a number of ghost stories he had heard during the fifty years he had spent at Buckfast Abbey. These included the tale of a 'courteous monk' who had been seen by a member of the congregation singing with the choir and bowing to the Abbot throughout the service. By far the most intriguing abbey apparition is the occasional appearance of Richard Coer de Lion (1157-1199) clad in shining armour, charging through the church astride his trusty steed in pursuit of a fleeing maiden.

Richard the Lionheart.

Historically, there is an important link between the Plantagenet monarch and the abbey, for on 18 November 1189, two months after his Coronation in succession to his father Henry II; Richard, King of England, Count of Anjou, Duke of Normandy and Aquitaine, exempted the monks of Buckfast Abbey from all forms of taxation and granted a royal charter proclaiming: 'Know ye that we for the love of God and for the safety of our soul and all our ancestors and successors, have conceded and by this present deed have confirmed to God and the Blessed Mary of Bocfast and to the monks serving there all the donations which have been reasonably made to them, in lands and tenures and tenements, in free and perpetual almonry'.

Dartmouth harbour from where the third crusade began.

A few months after making this generous gift, vessels assembled at Warfleet Creek, Dartmouth, before embarking on the king's third crusade to the Holy Land. Richard had taken an oath on the cross to devote his life to liberate Jerusalem from the Saracens. The Lionheart's macho image and his courage in battle belied the fact that he had homosexual tendencies. In 1191 he consented to his mother's wishes and got married in Cyprus to Princess Berengaria (1163-1230), daughter of the King of Navarre, although it seems that his choice of bride was influenced by the striking resemblance she bore to her brother Sancho with whom he had earlier embarked upon a torrid affair. Although, it is known that Richard fathered an illegitimate child, historians are reasonably certain that the union with Berengaria was never consummated. She was treated courteously by Richard and allowed to accompany her husband throughout the Crusade but she remains the only Queen of England never to have set foot in this country.

The Crusaders failed in their quest and eventually negotiated an uneasy truce with Saracen warlord Saladin. When Richard's party left the Holy Land to return home in October 1192, the ladies sailed on a different vessel to the King who was shipwrecked in the Adriatic. He then set out overland across Europe until he was captured and flung into a dungeon by the Duke of Austria, whom he had publicly disgraced in the Holy Land by accusing him of insubordination and having his banner trampled in the dirt. Romantic legend relates how the place of imprisonment was located by his devoted minstrel Blondel who travelled throughout Austria singing songs he had written with the king until the monarch joined in the refrain from behind a barred window. A huge ransom was demanded and the monks of Buckfast donated the proceeds of a year's sale of local wool towards the cost of obtaining Richard's release.

The ruins of Buckfast Abbey.

Following the king's return to London in March 1194, he made no attempt to rejoin the queen abroad until he was taken to task by a brave monk who reminded him of the fate of Sodom. This rebuke brought about a brief reunion of the couple during Christmas 1196. Three years later, the Lionheart attempted to regain lands he had lost on the Continent. Besieging a town he recklessly rode up to the walls in full view of the defenders and was hit in the right shoulder by a crossbow bolt. Richard's forces fought on to victory and the victim sent for the bowman, praised him on the accuracy of his marksmanship and granted him a pardon. However, the royal physician forfeited his life when he made a hash of removing the arrow and the wound turned gangrenous. Several days later, the king succumbed in agony. Following her husband's death, Queen Berengaria received the revenues from the tin mines of Devon and Cornwall. She used her wealth to found and live at the Abbey of L'Epau in Le Mans, which fell into ruin after her death in 1230. A gruesome discovery was made in the Seventeenth Century when the mutilated effigy and remains of the Queen were found on the site of the old Abbey graveyard beneath a pile of wheat.

In 1882, a group of Benedictine monks driven out of France during the revolution from land once owned by Richard I, accepted favourable terms to relocate to Buckfastleigh. The abbey site had been vacated following the dissolution of the monasteries ordered by Henry VIII in 1539. In a testament of faith the monks began to rebuild the church in 1906. Starting with £5 in the kitty and a supply of sand from a local farmer the new place of worship reached completion in 1938. There are various explanations for the appearance of the ghost of Richard the Lionheart. It may be that his spirit is still trying to rid himself of his unwanted bride and haunting the abbey as a reprisal against the monk who dared to chide him over his sexual preferences, or, perhaps he is attempting to prevent his queen's tormented soul, having been disturbed in her final resting place, from seeking refuge in the abbey whose future he secured for the monks of Buckfast.

Alternatively, it has been suggested that the knight in shining armour, far from being Richard the Lionheart, is more than likely the figment of the imagination of someone who sampled rather too much of Buckfast Abbey's world famous tonic wine!

SIR JOHN HOLLAND

The Jousting Ghost of Dartington

Devon's most elegant medieval manor, Dartington Hall, was built in the Fourteenth Century for the Duke of Exeter, John Holland (c1352-1400). Following the death of his father Thomas Holland, the first Earl of Kent, his mother Joan, known as the 'Fair Maid of Kent', became the wife of Edward, the Black Prince. Consequently when the couple had a child, Thomas Holland became half-brother to a future sovereign – King Richard II.

When Richard succeeded to the throne at the age of ten in 1377, he came under the influence of his scheming uncle John of Gaunt, the Duke of Lancaster who had designs on the crown. According to unsubstantiated rumour, this was to lead to a conflict of loyalties for John Holland who married the duke's daughter. In 1384, a friar informed Richard that Lancaster was plotting to dethrone him. The duke convinced the king that the monk was lying and suggested that his accuser should be held in detention by Holland while the matter was investigated. Once in custody, it has been suggested that Holland himself gave the order for the prisoner to be butchered in his cell whilst being 'questioned'.

There is absolutely no doubt that John Holland's violent temper led him to commit cold-blooded murder a year later. Whilst accompanying King Richard on a journey to Scotland, one of his squires was killed near York in a quarrel with an archer in the employ of Ralph, the eldest son of the Earl of Stafford. The next evening, Ralph rode to visit Holland to appease him for the outrage whilst simultaneously, Holland was riding out to demand an explanation of Stafford. As they met in the dark, Holland shouted, 'Who goes by?' and upon hearing the reply 'Stafford', plunged his sword into the unsuspecting nobleman before fleeing from the scene of the crime and seeking sanctuary in a church. The Earl of Stafford demanded vengeance for the unprovoked attack on his son and King Richard complied by ordering Holland's lands to be seized. Their mother implored the king to grant a pardon to

Dartington Hall.

Holland and fell ill and died of grief when her request was refused.

Following this tragic turn of events, the king relented whilst in mourning for his mother and Holland was whisked out of the country to take part in the campaign in Spain under the command of his father-in-law. Holland, a renowned jouster who had won many tournaments, quickly restored his reputation by performing numerous acts of valour on the battlefield. On his return to England, he regained the royal favour and was appointed life Chamberlain of England. In 1397, further honours were heaped upon him after he had assisted his half-brother to put down a conspiracy against the crown by a group of lords. Now, at the height of his powers he was created Duke of Exeter, a title in the county where he had previously been granted lands and built his sumptuous mansion at Dartington.

However, this success was to prove short-lived, for when the king's opponent the Duke of Lancaster died in 1399 his lands were confiscated by the king, provoking his equally ambitious son Henry to snatch the crown at an opportune moment whilst King Richard and John Holland were on an expedition to Ireland. Richard gave himself up, was forced to abdicate and although there is no evidence to support the theory that he was murdered as represented in Shakespeare's classic play *Richard II*, it is believed that he starved himself to death whilst held in prison at Pontefract.

John Holland was deprived of his lands and dukedom of Devon but his life was spared and after answering charges satisfactorily, he was released, but a few months before Richard's death, he became implicated in a failed plot to overthrow his brother-in-law Henry IV and restore his half-brother to the throne. He was captured at Pleshey and immediately executed at the behest of the Countess of Hereford, whose husband had been one of the lords earlier involved in intrigue against the crown and sent into exile by Richard. According to the quaint custom of the day, Holland's head was put on public display, before his widow successfully appealed to her brother for it's removal and the king ordered the head to be delivered to the 'master or keeper of the college of the church of Plessey' where it was laid to rest with his body.

Holland's lands and honours were initially confiscated but later restored to the family. His second son, John, regained the title of Duke of Exeter and continued to reside at Dartington Hall where he had been born in 1395. Soon, the servants of his household were petrified by the sounds of knights on horse-back in the tilting yard. For, late at night they were convinced that the ghost of John Holland took part in his favourite pastime finding worthy opponents to joust with in the spirit world!

THE DUKE OF SOMERSET & LADY JANE SEYMOUR

The Protectors of Berry Pomeroy

The Duke of Somerset, Edward Seymour (c1506-1552), had recently been appointed Protector of the Realm, with full authority to conduct affairs of state on behalf of his youthful nephew, King Edward VI, when he acquired Berry Pomeroy in 1547. The previous owner, staunch Roman Catholic Sir Thomas Pomeroy, was arrested two years later for his role in the Western Rebellion. In an act of treason, he helped to raise an army of 10,000 Devonians and led them into battle in protest against church reforms introduced by the Calvinist Protector. Nevertheless, Seymour treated Pomeroy mercifully and ordered his release, unlike four of his fellow conspirators who paid the full penalty for their actions and were hung, drawn and quartered.

Thomas Pomeroy was indeed fortunate, for Protector Somerset acted ruthlessly when his authority was challenged by his own brother Thomas Seymour. The warring siblings' influence in royal circles had come about through the marriage of their sister Jane Seymour (1509-1537), who became the third wife of King Henry VIII. A former lady in waiting to Catherine of Aragon and Anne Boleyn, Jane succeeded where her predecessors had failed in satisfying the monarch's obsession with providing a male heir but died in the process of delivering their son, Edward. To marry Jane, Henry broke away from Rome, founded the Church of England, then had his marriage to Anne Boleyn annulled before ordering her execution on charges of adultery and incest with her brother.

Following the death of 'Bluff King Hal' in 1547, Thomas Seymour, Lord Admiral of England, had a proposal of marriage rejected by the advisors of Princess Elizabeth, Henry's thirteen-year-old daughter by the ill-fated Anne Boleyn, then outraged his brother by marrying Catherine Parr, the sixth wife and widow of Henry VIII, whilst the country was still in mourning for the monarch.

Berry Pomeroy Castle.

When Catherine died in childbirth a year later, Thomas wasted no time in trying to strengthen his standing at court by renewing his attempts to obtain the hand of Elizabeth who remained unmarried and was dubbed the 'Virgin Queen'. Thomas also tried to usurp his brother by trying to arrange a marriage between his ward Jane Grey and King Edward when the children were barely ten years old. The Protector had similar plans for his own daughter and the young king and resented this obvious threat to his royal authority. Despite pleading with Thomas to abandon his intrigues and ambitions, he could not dissuade his brother from further involvement in a plot to oust him from office. This latest affront could not be overlooked and Edward had no hesitation in sanctioning the trial and resultant execution of his unrepentant brother in 1549.

However, even this drastic course action did not protect Seymour from his enemies for long. Soon after quelling the Western Rebellion, he was toppled from power by John Dudley, the Duke of Northumberland. He pleaded guilty to numerous charges of profiting from the dissolution of monasteries and sale of church lands and received a full pardon. Despite an uneasy alliance forged by the marriage of Somerset's daughter to Northumberland's son in 1551, Seymour was arrested six months later for allegedly plotting to murder his archrival Dudley. The prisoner was conveyed along the River Thames from the Tower to Westminster and tried by his peers. He was acquitted of treason but condemned to death for felony – charges relating to Somerset's debts to the young king. Seymour still enjoyed popular support and a contemporary source reported that the people 'supposing he had been clerely quitte, when they see the axe of the Tower put downe, made much a shryke and castinge up of caps, that it was heard into the Long Acre beyond Charinge Crosse' and on his way back to the Tower they cried, 'God Save Him'.

Because of the wide-held sympathy for Seymour, an order was given for the public to stay away from the place of execution at Tower Hill, but this was ignored and a huge crowd gathered to witness the event. With great dignity, Seymour pronounced his loyalty to the king, and then calmly laid his head on the block. As the executioner's axe fell his supporters surged forward to dip their handkerchiefs in his blood. Seymour was buried in the Tower of London between Anne Boleyn and Catherine Howard, the two unfortunate wives of Henry VIII who had also suffered the unkindest cut!

Lady Jane Seymour.

The Protector's lands were confiscated but later restored to the Seymour family who deserted Berry Pomeroy following the death of the third baronet in 1688. According to a colourful choice of local legends, the castle fell into ruin following an artillery bombardment during the Civil War or was destroyed by a lightning induced fire during a terrible thunderstorm. Whatever the truth, it seems that the only inhabitants of the castle since those times are numerous ghosts who are regularly seen – or in the case of a servant's illegitimate crying baby said to have been smothered soon after birth – heard. In 1968, the Psychic Research Society confirmed that holiday snaps taken by a visitor were genuine and revealed the ghostly images of a medieval woman and a man. At the time these were thought to be of Lady Margaret Pomeroy, who was locked up and left to die of starvation by her jealous sister, and Sir Thomas Pomeroy, wrongly supposed by many writers to have forfeited his lands and been executed whilst the Lord Protector was in power. Clearly, this was a case of mistaken identity as the castle owner who met this tragic fate was of course, Edward Seymour himself, apparently installed in the hereafter with his head intact, accompanied by his sister Jane, in their new roles as the Protectors of Berry Pomeroy.

LADY JANE GREY

The Nine Days Queen of Boringdon Hall

Henry VIII's six marriages produced three monarchs. Daughters, who earned his displeasure and the disposal of their mothers, produced two queens – Mary I and Elizabeth I. Despite being branded illegitimate by their father, they were each to be handed an opportunity in the wake of a sole male heir – the sickly Edward VI who succeeded to the throne in 1547 at the age of nine. Six years later as he lay dying of consumption, he was persuaded by his chief advisers to pass over the claims of his half-sisters and four other possible claimants to the throne and nominate his first cousin as the next in line. Totally oblivious to this development, sixteen year-old Lady Jane Grey (1537-1554) swooned when told that Edward had succumbed and she had been proclaimed monarch. However, her reign was to be briefest in England's history and she is forever remembered as the 'Nine Days Queen'.

Granddaughter of Henry VIII's younger sister Mary, Lady Jane became an unwitting political pawn in a dynastic power game. When barely nine, she entered the household of Henry's widow, Catherine Parr and was chief mourner when her mistress died two years later in 1548. Catherine's second husband, Lord Admiral of England, Thomas Seymour, then purchased the wardship of Jane from her parents, a distasteful but common practice which gave him the right to administer Jane's estate, also enabling him to profit politically and financially by determining whom she would marry. Seymour planned to use his influence to arrange a betrothal between Jane and Edward VI. However, his brother, Edward Seymour, owner of Totnes and Berry Pomeroy Castle, was zealously planning a union between the young king and his own daughter, whilst hoping to marry off Jane to his eldest son. The scheming brothers' plans to gain control of the kingdom resulted from the fact that their sister Jane Seymour had died giving birth to Edward VI. Edward Seymour took advantage of this family connection to become the power behind the throne as Lord Protector – effectively ruling the country on behalf of his royal brother-in-law. He dealt with the threat from the palace intrigues of Thomas by reluctantly authorising his headstrong brother's execution. However, Edward had made many other enemies in court circles, which cost him his own life when he was also beheaded on trumped-up charges of treason.

Following the fall of the Seymours, Lady Jane's father, the Duke of Suffolk, then allied himself with the ambitious John Dudley, Duke of Northumberland – a powerful member of the Privy Council who had overthrown and succeeded Edward Seymour. Northumberland obtained the king's sanction for his son Guildford Dudley to marry Jane in 1553. The match was made against her will and she only went through with the ceremony after threatened with violence by her father. The stress she suffered quickly brought on a serious illness that almost proved fatal. This union was a plot to alter the succession from the Tudors to the Dudleys, which Edward VI readily accepted because he felt closer to Jane, than his half-sisters Mary and Elizabeth. The rightful heir was Mary, Henry VIII's eldest daughter by Catherine of Aragon, who evaded a kidnap attempt by Northumberland before her supporters mounted a successful armed rising. Jane and her husband were arrested and consigned to the Tower of London. Pleading guilty to high treason they were sentenced to death. Queen Mary was disposed to extend mercy until Jane's father foolishly participated in a revolt of Kent peasants led by Sir Thomas Wyatt following the announcement that Mary would marry the Roman Catholic, Philip of Spain. Any further Protestant insurgence was discouraged by 'Bloody Mary' who snuffed out any remaining

Lady Jane Grey.

threat from subjects loyal to Jane. Sixty people were executed including Jane's father and father-in-law. Resigned to her fate, Jane refused to see her husband on the morning of their execution, lest the meeting disturb 'the holy tranquillity with which they had prepared themselves for death'. However, when escorted to the scaffold she was cruelly exposed to the bleeding, headless body of her luckless spouse before she too, knelt beneath the shadow of the executioner's axe. From the scaffold, she made a speech asserting that she had never desired the crown and that she was to die 'a true Christian woman'.

Medieval tales relate how the ghost of Lady Jane roamed the grounds of Boringdon Hall, at Colebrook, Plympton. It was the family home where she had spent a happy and contented childhood until her destiny was sealed when she was compelled to leave Devon to enter the service of Catherine Parr. More disturbing is the spirit of Jane's serving maid who walks the staircase and corridors of the manor that is now a hotel. It is said that she foresaw her mistress's fate and her appearances always signal impending disaster for the owners. Such a case occurred in the 1980s when the spectral maid was seen weeping, covering her face with her hands shortly before a serious fire broke out. Deeply affected by this incident, the owner felt he had disregarded her warning and immediately sold the Hall.

SIR FRANCIS DRAKE

In League With the Devil

Devon folklore, traditions and ghost stories abound concerning the immortal Elizabethan hero who became a legend in his own lifetime – Sir Francis Drake (c1549-1596). The adventurer's triumphs included circumnavigating the globe in 1581, for which, he was knighted by Queen Elizabeth I on board his vessel the Golden Hind. He boasted of 'singeing the King of Spain's beard' during a daring raid which destroyed thirty vessels in the port of Cadiz in 1587 and, a year later, defeated the might of the Spanish Armada after coolly completing a game of bowls on Plymouth Hoe. His final mission proved something of an anticlimax to his glittering career. With a distinguished relative, Sir John Hawkins, they launched a disastrous campaign on the Spanish Maine. Both of the old seadogs succumbed through illness during the voyage and were buried at sea.

Born at Crowndale Farm, near Tavistock, Drake's international reputation did not prevent him from representing his county in the House of Commons and serving Plymouth as Lord Mayor. According to one tall story, an act of witchcraft enabled him to supply the city with water from Dartmoor when he muttered some words of magic over a stream and the leat followed him back to the gates of the city. Similar tales included how Drake had whittled on a stick at Devil's Point in Plymouth Sound. As each shaving fell on the water it was transformed into a fire ship, which caused havoc amongst the Spanish Armada. Many people believed that Drake was in league with the Devil. However, pact or no pact, 'Old Nick' was driven off when he tried to interfere with building work on Drake's home at Buckland Abbey. On this occasion Drake proved that he feared the Devil no more than Dons. Even his love life was given a supernatural twist, for it was told that whilst harrying Hispanic vessels, the lady betrothed to him, fearing him dead, gave her hand to another suitor. As the

Drake battles the Armada off Plymouth.

wedding party entered the Somerset church, a cannon ball fell just short of the building, like a shot across the bows of the bridegroom, warning him that Drake was very much alive and knew precisely what was transpiring on dry land. The shocked bride, Elizabeth Sydenham, called off the wedding and in due course became Drake's wife.

The ghost of Francis Drake haunts the vicinity of Exeter Cathedral. It is believed that he used to meet up nearby with fellow Elizabethan sea captains at the Ship Inn, where his mischievous spirit continues to make its presence firmly felt by helping people unceremoniously down the stairs with an invisible push in the back. In Victorian times, his apparition was reportedly haunting the grounds of Nutwell, Lympstone, Many of the family servants admitted that they were terrified whenever they had the 'honour' of meeting the Elizabethan hero, but one man boasted of how he had turned the tables on Drake. Returning at midnight to the manor from an inn, where conviviality had been the order of the evening, he related how he was walking 'as straight as a chalk line' when he was suddenly accosted by the figure of Sir Francis who drew his sword and approached him menacingly. The unwelcome visitor allegedly fled and was never seen again when the inebriated servant refused to cow and shouted, 'Boo, Hoo!'

Along with King Arthur, Francis Drake is credited with leading the Wisht Hunt on Dartmoor, accompanied by spectral hounds with eyes of fire; he rides in a black carriage pulled by four headless horses. This association with the nation's heroic figures is continued by the legend of Drake's Drum. Through the ages, many Devonians have believed that the Elizabethan adventurer is reincarnated in each succeeding naval hero such as Blake and Nelson. For, according to tradition, when Drake was on the point of death he made a promise to return whenever his country was threatened. In Henry Newbolt's famous poem 'Drake's Drum' the 'Capten' will 'quit the port of heaven' to fight the enemy and 'drum them up the Channel as we drummed them long ago'.

The instrument in question is believed to have 'accompanied' Drake on his voyage around the world and plays a ghostly tattoo without the aid of human hands to summon Drake from eternity. Hanging on the wall of Drake's old Somerset home at Combe Sydenham, it was said to have signalled the outbreak of World War One. Then, mysteriously, in 1918, when the Germans surrendered at Scapa Flow and the British Grand Fleet surrounded the enemy vessels, sailors heard a drum roll at intervals in the flagship until the fleet dropped anchor. Although the commander twice sent men to see who was beating it, and himself made a personal investigation, every man was found to be dutifully positioned at his battle station and no drummer was ever discovered. Word spread like wildfire among the crews that Drake's drum had performed a victory roll!

SIR BERNARD & DAME GERTRUDE DRAKE

The Betrayed Spirits of Musbury

The Drake Memorial at St Michael's Church, Musbury, is the focal point of East Devon's most eerie ghost story. The impressive stone sculpture features three life-size couples, kneeling and holding prayer books. They are members of the Drake family whose family seat was at the nearby mansion of Ashe House. Locals say that at the stroke of midnight, the statues come to life and the spirits of the long departed rise up and walk, two by two, out of the churchyard and down to the nearby stream, where they take a refreshing drink before returning to their devotions at the monument!

The central figures of the memorial represent Sir Bernard Drake (died 1586), accompanied by his loyal wife Dame Gertrude (died 1601), the daughter of Bartholomew Fortescue of Fileigh. The monument depicts two more generations of the Drake family, Bernard and Gertrude's eldest son and their daughter-in-law, John and Dorothy, together with Bernard's parents, John and Amy – whose marriage had united two of Devon's greatest seafaring families. The groom was related to the illustrious Francis Drake, whilst the bride was a kinsman of Richard Grenville. Sir Bernard and Dame Gertrude had six children and one of their great-granddaughters, Elizabeth, married Member of Parliament Sir Winston Churchill. The eldest son of this union, John, was born at Ashe in 1650 and was created the first Duke of Marlborough in 1702 before distinguishing himself as one of England's greatest generals, leading allied victories over the French at Bleineim, Ramillies and Oudenaarde. The illustrious descendants of this branch of the family include the man recently voted the greatest Briton of all time, Sir Winston Churchill, the nation's inspirational Prime Minister during the dark days of the Second World War (1939-45).

The coat of arms of Francis Drake.

The most famous tale associated with Sir Bernard Drake concerns an alleged, but unsubstantiated, disagreement with his distant cousin Sir Francis Drake, which resulted in a confrontation at court when he soundly 'boxed the ears' of his renowned kinsman. Tradition relates that after Drake was knighted on board the Golden Hind by Queen Elizabeth I – in honour of his epic voyage around the world in 1581 – he sought to design a coat-of-arms to match his elevated status in life, therefore, he assumed the armorial bearings of the Drakes of Ashe. Far from pleased with being associated with the great navigator, Sir Bernard considered his namesake an upstart and was infuriated as he considered the family relationship to be somewhat tenuous. Upon hearing of this slight upon one of her personal favourites, the Queen bestowed upon Sir Francis a completely 'new coat of everlasting honour, to himself and posterity' portraying a ship drawn around the world with a rope guided by the hand of God emerging from a cloud. Purportedly, an act of derision contained in the crest is the armorial bearing of the Drakes of Ashe; a mythical monster called a wyvern is shown hanging upside down in the rigging.

Bernard Drake was a fearless naval commander who was knighted by the sovereign four years after Sir Francis in 1585. He had pleased the Queen by completing a successful mission 'to proceed to Newfoundland to warn the English engaged in the fisheries there of the seizure of English ships in Spain, and to seize all ships in Newfoundland belonging to the King Of Spain or any of his subjects, and to bring them into some of the western ports of England without dispersing any part of their lading until further orders'.

On his return, Drake put in at Dartmouth with a Portuguese man 'o' war called the *Lion of Viana* that he had seized off the coast of Brittany. Unfortunately, the moment of his greatest triumph was to inadvertently bring about his premature death. For, the captured crew were transported to Exeter Castle where they were held in custody to await trial at the forthcoming Spring Assizes. After rotting for some months in the inhumane conditions of an Elizabethan prison cell, it is clear that they had contracted some terrible contagious disease, perhaps cholera or typhoid, for when they were brought up before the court, contemporary accounts record that, 'suddenly there arose such a noisom smell from the bar, that a great number of the people there present were therewith infected; whereof in a short time after, died the said judge, Sir John Chicester, Sir Arthur Bassett and Sir Bernard Drake, Knights and Justices of the Peace, then setting on the Bench; and eleven of the jury impanelled, the twelfth man only escaping; with divers other persons'.

Apparently, such afflictions were an occupational hazard for courts, as the philosopher Francis Bacon succinctly observed, 'The most pernicious infection, next the plague, is the smell of the goal, when prisoners have been long, and close, and nastily kept; whereof we have had in our time experience twice or thrice, when both the judges that sat upon the goal, and numbers of those that attended the business, sickened upon it, and died. Out of question, most dangerous is the smell of man's flesh or sweat putrefied; for they are not those stinks which the nostrils straight abhor and expel, that are the most pernicious; but such airs as have some similitude with man's body; and so insinuate themselves, and betray the spirits'.

Fatally stricken, Sir Bernard attempted to make his way home to Musbury, before his strength gave out at Crediton, where he was buried in the churchyard. His 'betrayed spirit' rejoins the bosom of his family at Musbury to take their evening constitutional together.

SIR HUMPREY GILBERT

The Father of Colonisation

Elizabethan soldier and explorer Sir Humphrey Gilbert (1539-1583) was born at Greenway Court, Galmpton. His mother was the twice-married Katherine Champernowne of Modbury. According to legend, when Humphrey's younger half-brother Sir Walter Raleigh first introduced tobacco in England and was demonstrating the art of pipe-smoking to him at the ancestral home on the River Dart, the sight of burning alarmed a servant who threw a jug of ale in the startled smoker's face in a misguided attempt to put out the fire!

Educated at Eton and Oxford, Gilbert embarked upon a military career in the service of Princess Elizabeth through the influence of his aunt, Katherine Ashley, the governess of the future monarch. During the 1560s he distinguished himself in the field, then gained notoriety in Ireland when appointed military commander of Munster where he ruthlessly crushed uprisings and refused to negotiate with rebels unless they first submitted to him, swore an oath of allegiance to the queen and pledged to abide by the law. Those who surrendered to these terms were forced to make a terrifying march along a corridor lined with rows of the decapitated heads of former dissidents.

In 1571, Gilbert was returned to Parliament as member for Plymouth and turned his ambitions to exploration, advocating the case to search for a trade route via a northwest passage over America to the Pacific Ocean and plans for the colonisation of the New World to alleviate the rising tide of vagrancy and poverty in the mother country. In 1578, Gilbert took part in a joint venture with Walter Raleigh plundering Spanish vessels for treasure. Having proved his worth at sea, he immediately received a royal patent to seek 'remote heathen and barbarous lands'. After various schemes foundered through lack of finance, he finally gained sufficient support to set sail on a doomed quest with a fleet of five ships – the *Delight*, the *Bark Raleigh*, the *Golden Hind*, the *Swallow* and the *Squirrel*. Leaving from Plymouth early in June 1583, the expedition sighted Newfoundland by the end of July, having already suffered the loss of the *Bark Raleigh*, which had turned back through a lack of provisions. Entering the harbour of St John's, Gilbert claimed all land within a 200 leagues radius in the name of the sovereign Queen Elizabeth. He also imposed his authority on the local fishermen by securing promises of fees payable to him in return for leases for the continued use of fishing grounds. In

Sir Humphrey Gilbert.

Greenway Court (right) on the River Dart.

late August, the captain of the *Swallow* refused to follow Gilbert any further, preferring to return to England while the three remaining ships set off on a reconnaissance southwards along the coast to Sable Island. Within days, the *Delight* ran aground and sank, taking with her a collection of mineral specimens and newly charted maps of the sea route. Panic swept through the superstitious crews of the two surviving ships who now feared for their own lives. Their concerns were appeased when a decision was taken to abandon the mission and sail back to England. Gilbert was confident that his relevant success would attract royal patronage to mount larger expeditions to explore the Americas – little realising that this was to be his final voyage. Having encountered a fierce squall rounding the Azores, his ship the *Squirrel* was engulfed by the sea and sank beneath mountainous waves. The captain of the *Golden Hind* reported that Sir Humphrey was last seen on deck calmly reading a book and reassuring his crew as the terrible storm raged: 'We are as near to heaven by seas as by land'.

Raleigh Gilbert, Humphrey's son, took up his father's dream of conquering the New World, and succeeded in establishing a colony on the coast of Maine. Although the venture had to be abandoned within a year, following a severe winter which brought about the deaths of many of the 120 settlers, an inscription on the landing site records his achievement: 'The first colony on the shores of New England was founded here August 19, 1607'.

Remembered as a tragic hero and the 'Father of Colonisation', Sir Humphrey Gilbert had a strong affinity with the occult and wrote that he had experienced 'strong visions' between February and April 1567. These apparitions laden with symbolic dragons, angels and archaic lore pointed to a life of greatness and, in a strange contrast to the conditions he imposed when receiving the submission of Irish rebels, he saw himself splendidly dressed and fully armed receiving the homage of non other than the manifestations of biblical characters Solomon and Job who promised to guide him with their wisdom and impart mystical secrets. Cast adrift in the hereafter, the forlorn ghost of Sir Humphrey was frequently spotted by his servants roaming around his former home. Thwarted from pursuing his goals in life, his restless spirit sought the refuge and comfort of Greenway Court until it was demolished and replaced by a Georgian mansion. From 1938 until her death in 1976, the house was the much loved summer residence of the world's most popular mystery writer Agatha Christie and has now passed into the custodianship of the National Trust.

SIR WALTER RALEIGH

The Search for El Dorado

Brilliant courtier, parliamentarian, businessman, soldier, seaman, coloniser, explorer, scientist, philosopher, historian and poet, Walter Raleigh (c1552-1618) was one of the most celebrated men of the Elizabethan age. His achievements outstripped those of his illustrious half-brother Sir Humphrey Gilbert, 'The Father of Colonisation', who was lost at sea whilst returning from a voyage of discovery to Newfoundland.

Born at Hayes Barton, East Budleigh, Raleigh tried to emulate his half-brother by organising attempts to set up English colonies in North America. He won favour with Queen Elizabeth by naming Virginia in honour of the monarch known as the 'Virgin Queen'. In return 'Good Queen Bess' bestowed a knighthood on Raleigh and enabled him to become one of the richest men in England when she granted him lucrative monopolies in the wine and cloth trade. Administrative posts were obtained in Devon where he was appointed Vice-admiral, Warden of the Stannaries, and also represented the county in the House of Commons. In 1585, Raleigh authorised an expedition led by his cousin Sir Richard Grenville (destined to die eleven years later on board the *Revenge* in a heroic sea-

The birthplace of Walter Raleigh at Hayes Barton

battle with the Spanish). Sailing from Bideford to Roanoke Island, off the coast of what is now North Carolina, Grenville put men ashore to prepare a colony.

A year later Francis Drake rescued them after they had survived food shortages and skirmishes with the native Americans. A further attempt to inhabit the island ended in mystery when a hundred men, women and children disappeared without trace. The only clue to their whereabouts was a word carved in the bark of a tree, which indicated they might have moved to a nearby island 'CROATOAN'. A search party could find no sign of life there, but a century later, grey-eyed Indians told of grandparents who could 'talk in a book' and related tales of a ghostly vessel called 'Sir Walter Raleigh's Ship' that appeared sometimes offshore – always 'under sail, in a gallant posture'.

The death of Queen Elizabeth in 1603 brought about a dramatic change in Raleigh's fortunes. His enemies at court spread rumours that he was opposed to the accession of King James. The new monarch immediately ordered his arrest and Raleigh was tried for treason, declared guilty and sentenced to death. On the eve of the execution he was granted a reprieve and committed to the Tower of London. Here, he was allowed special privileges; living in relative comfort accompanied by his wife, son and personal servants, but was held for thirteen years. During his captivity, he conducted scientific experiments and undertook a daunting literary work *The History of the World*.

In 1616, he was released and given an opportunity to redeem himself by undertaking an expedition to the Orincho River in Venezuela to search for gold, promising to find evidence of the legendary El Dorado. He was now over sixty and fell ill in Trinidad, which he had claimed for the crown twenty years earlier. The rest of the party carried on without him but suffered many losses when they landed on Spanish territory and were apprehended by a patrol. Raleigh's son Wat was killed and the second-in-command was so ashamed of the failure that he stabbed himself in the heart. The expedition returned to England in disgrace and Raleigh poured out his despair in a letter to his wife, comparing his dilemma with that faced by two of Devon's most famous seafarers: 'As Sir Francis Drake and Sir John Hawkins died broken-hearted when they failed of their enterprise, I would willingly do the like, did I not contend against sorrow, in hope to provide somewhat for you

Sir Walter Raleigh.

in comfort'. On his return to London, the Spanish ambassador demanded that Raleigh should die and King James complied with the request. For the last time he was escorted to the Tower. Brushing aside thoughts of suicide he resolved 'to die in the light not in the darkness'. On the scaffold, Raleigh's final impassioned speech lasted for forty-five minutes. He declined the offer of a blindfold, 'Think you I fear the shadow of the axe, when I fear not the axe itself?' he enquired. 'What dost thou fear?' urged the prisoner, 'Strike, man, strike!' The executioner was totally unnerved by the victim's calm demeanour and required two swings of the axe to sever the head from the body.

Raleigh's ghost has appeared at various West Country locations connected with his life. In Cornwall, it is claimed that the first tobacco to be smoked in England was enjoyed at Penzance where regulars of the Dolphin Inn claim Walter's spirit is present, as they frequently smell the smoke from his pipe. Raleigh resided at Sherbourne Castle, Dorset, which he haunts each year on 29 September – the eve of the feast of St

Michael the Archangel – the leader of the heavenly armies in their battle against the forces of Hell. After walking peacefully under the trees, he sits below a tree dubbed 'Raleigh's Oak' then vanishes. Fittingly, in Devon, his frequent presence is warmly felt by the regulars at an inn, named in his honour and situated near his birthplace at East Budleigh – the Sir Walter Raleigh.

KING CHARLES I & QUEEN HENRIETTA MARIA

Martyrs of the Civil War

The Martyr King, Charles I (1600-1649) stubbornly refused to abide by the decisions of Parliament and governed the country as a virtual dictator for eleven years. Matters were brought to a head in 1640, when he entered the House of Commons with an armed guard seeking to arrest five Members of Parliament, thereby plunging England into a calamitous Civil War. Cavaliers and Roundheads struggled for supremacy resulting in an overwhelming defeat for the Royalists by Oliver Cromwell's New Model Army at the Battle of Naseby in 1645. Charles' reign was brought to an end by the fall of the axe as he uttered his last word before entering eternity – 'Remember'.

Twenty years earlier, in the year of his succession to the throne and his marriage to Henrietta Marie of France (1609-1669), Charles journeyed to Devon to inspect the fleet and his army assembled at Plymouth. Bypassing Exeter, which was in the grip of the plague, his entourage made for Newton Abbot where the king was welcomed as the guest of Sir Richard Reynell at Forde House. No expense was spared as a sumptuous feast was provided. Following the fish course with a choice of mullets, gurnets, dories, peels, salmon and soles, meat dishes were served comprising of venison, mutton, veal and lamb. In addition the guests also consumed 140 partridges, 7 pheasants, 61 chickens, 46 capons, 10 ducks, 14 pullets, 6 geese, 71 turkeys, 28 pigeons, 1 peahen, two green plovers, 8 plovers, 1 gull, 36 larks, 38 rabbits and 1 hare! After dinner, Charles conferred knighthoods on three local men, two of who were the nephews of the king's host. The mansion is normally associated with the hasty tramping footsteps of a heavily booted ghost said to be William of Orange, whilst other guests swear that an unseen figure can be heard shuffling along the corridors with a noticeable limp, a trait endured by the physically deformed King Charles whose progress to his room was probably further impeded after devouring such an enormous meal!

Another incident that points to the ghostly presence of King Charles occurred in 1992, when Teignbridge Council commissioned the filming of a documentary covering the history of Forde House from the Sixteenth Century onwards. The filmmakers were dogged by an inexplicable series of technical difficulties that seriously held up progress. Various shots were set up and lit and seemed to be 'in the can' but failed to materialise as desired and had to be re-filmed. Also, three reels of videotape were 'mashed up' and rendered unusable. Things only improved when local members of the Sealed Knot Society arrived to re-enact scenes from the Civil War. Appropriately, they first feature in the film depicted as

King Charles inspecting his army at Plymouth.

ghostly figures from the past. However, even they did not totally escape the jinx. Virtually every print of a series of photographs taken for continuity purposes on location failed to develop.

Queen Henrietta Maria gave birth to the couple's ninth child in Devon at the height of the Civil War. On 3 April 1644, when seven months pregnant, the king compelled her to leave him in Oxford and make her way to the comparative safety of Exeter. The royal couple were fated never to see each other again. The Queen became seriously ill and the city was threatened with siege, yet, despite the dangers to her life she wrote to her husband from Exeter urging him not to worry and think only of his own safety: 'nothing is so much in my thoughts as what concerns your preservation, and that my own life is of very little consequence compared with that; for, as your affairs stand, they would be in danger if you come to help me, and I know that your affection would make you risk everything for that'.

Princess Henrietta Anne was delivered safely at Bedford House on 16 June. The baby was baptised by Dr Laurence Burnell a month later at a special font erected in Exeter Cathedral, but neither parent was in attendance. With Parliamentarian troops fast approaching the city and escape routes by sea from Plymouth or Torbay blocked by the enemy, the Queen scurried to Falmouth and sailed for the sanctuary of France. The baby princess was left in the care of the Exeter commander Sir John Berkley and conveyed to her mother in Paris when the city surrendered in April 1646. Queen Henrietta

Maria did not return from exile until after the Restoration when her son Charles II was crowned in 1660. Ten years later, her Devonian daughter died of peritonitis and the king presented a portrait of his late sister to the people of Exeter in recognition of the kindness they had shown to her at the start of her brief life.

The traumatic events surrounding the birth of her youngest child appears to have had a lasting impact on Queen Henrietta Maria whose spirit evidently continues to haunt Exeter. Between the two world wars, a lady visiting Bampfylde House overlooking the site of where Bedford House once stood, was overcome with sadness when she gazed out of the window whilst sitting in a Stuart period chair and saw a frail female figure dressed in Seventeenth Century costume. No-one else present could see what was upsetting her as she exclaimed, 'Oh the poor thing!' Had she witnessed the Queen searching for the child she had been forced to temporarily leave behind? In 1962, the figure of Henrietta Maria was positively identified in Exeter walking through the gardens of Barnfield House before she vanished into thin air before the eyes of an astonished onlooker. The ghost's careworn appearance matched Samuel Pepys description of the Queen prematurely aged by the loss of her beloved husband; 'she is a very little plain old woman, and nothing more in her presence in any respect nor garb than any ordinary woman'.

LADY MARY HOWARD & SIR RICHARD GRENVILLE

The Black Widow and the Black Pig

As the clock strikes midnight, the ghost of the Old Lady of Fitzford leaves Tavistock in a coach fashioned from the bones of the four husbands she survived. The skulls of her unfortunate suitors adorn each corner of the carriage, which is drawn by a headless horse. Travelling to Okehampton Castle, the cortege is accompanied by a sable hound with one eye in the middle of its forehead, which dutifully stoops at Okehampton Park to pluck a single blade of grass. This nightly ritual is the penance of Lady Mary Howard (1596-1671) whom posterity has falsely accused of murdering two or three of her four spouses.

Her reputation as a 'black widow' gained credence when she entered into marriage for a third time shortly after attaining her sixteenth birthday. Born Mary Fitz at Fitzford Manor, Tavistock, she inherited a fortune at the age of nine, when her father committed suicide after killing a man. Three years later she was plunged into an arranged marriage with Sir Allan Percy who immediately caught a fatal 'chill' whilst hunting. Aged fifteen, she eloped with Thomas Darcy whose unexplained death occurred a few months after the wedding. Her third marriage to Sir Charles Howard lasted ten years and produced two daughters before he too succumbed. Despite this unfortunate track record the heiress was still looked upon as 'a lady of extraordinary beauty' and 'the richest match in the West' when, in 1628, she entered into holy matrimony with Richard Grenville (1600-1659), namesake and grandson of the naval hero who had lost his life in an engagement against the Spanish on board the valiant *Revenge*.

Lady Mary Howard.

The bridegroom was heavily in debt as a result of his extravagant life-style and obviously regarded this marriage as an ideal opportunity to overcome his financial problems. However, the honeymoon period came to an abrupt end when Sir Richard discovered that his wife had astutely taken legal steps to prevent him gaining control of her riches. Violent quarrels ensued and on one occasion, whilst Lady Mary was expecting their second child, Grenville entered her bedchamber wielding a sword. Furthermore, he slandered her chief adviser and brother of her previous husband, the Earl of Suffolk, calling him 'a base lord'.

These incidents brought about an acrimonious divorce and numerous court appearances for Sir Richard who was ordered to pay crippling fines, alimony, costs and damages leading to imprisonment for non-payment. He was held at 'his majesty's pleasure' before escaping sixteen months later and sought refuge abroad in October 1633.

Despite these misdemeanours, Sir Richard retained the favour of King Charles I and returned from exile in 1639 to take up an army commission serving with distinction in Ireland. At the outset of the Civil War, he infuriated the Puritans when he hoodwinked them by offering his services to Cromwell, then switched sides once he had received outstanding arrears of back pay from Parliament. His effigy was hung from the gallows and a proclamation denounced Grenville as 'a traitor, rogue, villain and skellum'.

Sir Richard Grenville.

The king's reward for this cunning ploy was an appointment as Sheriff of Devon. With these powers Sir Richard seized his ex-wife's estates, whilst she was residing in London, on the grounds that she was a rebel. He also took the opportunity to exact a terrible revenge upon her supporters.

Lady Mary's solicitor was accused of being a spy and hanged without a hearing. Her land agent was flung into prison for six months until he was cleared of trumped up charges of sending money to Lady Mary to support the rebel cause. Unfortunately, he had contracted fever whilst awaiting trial and died shortly after his release. Dubbed 'The King's General in the West', Grenville became notorious for acts of brutality toward local people and the Puritan minister of Tavistock condemned the 'cursed cavaliers who thrust many of our poor neighbours into Lydford Castle'.

The atrocities that Sir Richard sanctioned have led many people to believe that the ghostly black pig that haunts the castle is the spirit of Grenville, although it is normally associated with the equally heartless Judge Jeffries who contrary to popular belief never actually held court at Lydford.

After failing to fulfil a rash promise in 1644 to break the siege of Plymouth 'by Christmas', Sir Richard was forced to retreat into Cornwall and Parliamentarian forces were ordered to advance upon 'Skellum Grenville's house at Tavistock'. Ignorant of the fact that the rightful owner was Lady Mary, the troops peppered the property with cannonballs and rounded up 120 prisoners before looting the mansion which according to a contemporary document contained 'excellent pillage for the soldiers ... £3000 in money and plate and other provisions in great quantity'.

Grenville's downfall was swift and brought about by his own arrogance. Relieved of his command, further arguments with his superiors and complaints about the sadistic treatment of his own troops, prisoners of war and country folk, led to his arrest and he was imprisoned at St Michael's Mount by order of the king. Roundhead forces captured Grenville's illegitimate son and executed him at Plymouth Garrison. Puritan newspapers trumpeted the death of 'Skellum Grenville's whelp' and Sir Richard realised that with a price on his head he could expect no mercy from the enemy if he fell into their hands and successfully appealed for his release. Heavily disguised, he sailed to Brest; finally settling in Ghent where, before his death, he bemoaned his fate in a self-pitying memoir entitled *Sir Richard Grenville's Defence against all Aspersions of Malignant Persons.*

THE DUKE OF MONMOUTH

The Pitchfork Rebellion

A national crisis was created by the death of King Charles II in February 1685, as he left no legitimate heir. James Scott, the Duke of Monmouth (1649-1685) was the eldest of several children conceived by the king's numerous mistresses, but his claims to the throne were ignored as Charles' younger brother James II overcame Parliament's concerns about his conversion to the Roman Catholic faith and was granted the succession.

Urged on by his Protestant supporters, Monmouth mounted an ill-fated challenge to wrest the crown from his uncle. With money raised from pawning the jewellery of his mistress, Lady Wentworth, the Monmouth Rebellion began in June 1685 with less than 100 men whose ranks swelled within a week to an estimated 4,000 when supporters in the West Country answered the call to arms. Recruitment began when Monmouth sailed from Holland and landed at Lyme Regis before crossing the border from Dorset into East Devon stopping at Axminster where he added to his force 'a great number of sober and pious men'.

The Devon Militia, mustered from Exeter to crush the rebellion, was led by Monmouth's old friend the Duke of Albermarle who received a letter from his 'cousin' proclaiming himself to be 'head of and captain-general of the protestant forces of this kingdom'. Sympathetic to the 'enemy' some militiamen, 'watching opportunities to leave their colours', deserted to join the cause, whilst the remainder did nothing to impede the progress of 'King Monmouth' and dropped back to shadow from a safe distance after almost crossing the path of the marching invasion force.

The Duke of Monmouth had been rapturously received during a tour of the South West five years earlier visiting Bristol, Bath, Taunton and Exeter – where reportedly about 1,000 'stout young men' greeted him. It was natural that he should return to the area for support in his foolhardy enterprise. Humble country folk happily supplied the charismatic duke with information, fighting men and provisions. The 'pitchfork rising' of tradesmen and farmers were largely non-conformist Puritan 'dissenters' opposed to both the Anglican church and the papist monarch but ill-equipped for war. Crucially, they did not have the support of the local gentry who were afraid to openly display what the Bishop of Exeter condemned as 'Hellish treason'. Consequently, when the rebels were intercepted in Somerset by the king's forces, the undisciplined ragbag army of yeomen were overrun at the Battle of Sedgemoor. Supplementing the royal

The Duke of Monmouth.

army were regiments loaned by William of Orange, the king's son-in-law who had his own designs on the Crown of England.

As half of his force were cut to pieces, the defeated Duke of Monmouth retreated hastily from the battlefield, but was pursued and caught hiding in a ditch disguised as a peasant in the New Forest. The 'Protestant Prince' tried to obtain belated favour from his uncle by offering to become a Catholic, but having had a price put on his head for declaring himself king, he was advised by the Earl of Dartmouth that a pardon was out of the question. Denied a trial, he was taken to Tower Hill where a shocked audience watched in horror as he was dispatched in grisly fashion by notorious executioner Jack Ketch. According to an eyewitness the axe-man failed with five attempts to decapitate the prisoner and 'severed not his head from his body till he cut it off with his knife'.

The Western Rebellion had been savagely crushed but the Duke quickly became a folk hero and within days of his unfortunate death, rumours began to circulate that he had avoided capture and the man who had been beheaded was one of five men chosen before Sedgemoor to impersonate Monmouth in order to confuse the enemy. Furthermore, having escaped from the battlefield it was only a matter of time before he would 'come again'. According to a contemporary account it was popularly believed among common folk that 'the Duke of Monmouth is not really dead, but only withdrawn until the harvest is over, and then his friends shall see him again in a much better condition than ever they did yet'.

Apparently, the handsome Duke did return to Devon in the afterlife, for whilst imprisoned with his family in the Tower of London, the Duke refuted an earlier claim that his mother Lucy Walters had secretly married King Charles giving him a 'legitimate and legal right' to the crown. This selfless act was designed to protect the lives of his wife and children, but he steadfastly refused to express any regret for his adulterous relationship with Lady Wentworth. As a result the church felt unable to administer the sacrament condemning his soul to roam eternity. The ghost of the Duke of Monmouth haunts the county along the Knight's Ride near Uplyme, riding a horse given to him by Edmund Prideaux, the owner of Ford Abbey, Thornecombe, where the Duke stayed whilst seeking support for a lost cause.

JUDGE JEFFRIES

The Black Pig of Lydford

Rebel supporters of the vanquished Duke of Monmouth fled from the Battle of Sedgemoor and sought sanctuary in the West Country where the government ordered them to be hunted down and brought before the notorious Judge George Jeffries (c1645-1689). Trials held in courts on the Western Circuit at Dorchester, Exeter, Taunton and Wells became infamous as the 'Bloody Assizes'.

Employing draconian measures calculated to strike fear into the local population who had supported insurrection, Jeffries savagely sentenced some 200 captured rebels to be executed. This gruesome business involved public hanging, burning of entrails, and the quartering of corpses, before boiling them in salt and dipping them in pitch to enable long term display. Heads were impaled on stakes and bleeding limbs were exhibited in parishes, which had supplied Monmouth with recruits. Hundreds of other prisoners were sold to plantation owners and transported to the colonies on slave ships such as the optimistically named *Happy Return*.

The corrupt judge also benefited financially by extorting money from a few well-connected prisoners. In exchange for a pardon, the son of Oliver Cromwell's Attorney General, Edmund Prideaux parted with £15,000. It seems his only 'crime' had been to receive the Duke of Monmouth and offer him the hospitality of his home near Axminster.

Charged with 'levying war against the king' or 'aiding and assisting the rebels against the king', prisoners at Dorchester were dealt with particularly harshly as Judge Jeffries was in severe discomfort troubled by gallstones that did little to improve his mood toward the accused. Following his black deeds in Dorset, the ghost of Judge Jeffries is said to haunt the Great House at Lyme Regis, which was then owned by a loyal supporter of the king who zealously assisted Judge Jeffries in his work of retribution in the aftermath of the rebellion. Although the Bishop of Exeter offered a £3 reward for information leading to the arrest of 'seditious fanatics' and ordered the clergy of his diocese to read out a declaration to their congregations condemning the rebels as 'a pestilential faction' which had to be rooted out by the sword of justice, the authorities in Devon were reluctant to arrest known rebels and a mere two dozen prisoners appeared before the judge. Another 343 were 'indicted of High Treason and still at large'

Judge George Jeffries.

and were to remain so until a General Pardon was granted a year later.

At Exeter Assizes the judge immediately ordered the execution of three men who had the temerity to plead innocence. Sentence of death was deferred on the remainder who admitted their guilt having been promised leniency for co-operating. However, this proved a false hope as they were denied the 'king's mercy' and ten more were hung, drawn and quartered whilst the remainder were exiled to servitude in the West Indies.

Bad memories of Judge Jeffries linger in the county through his spirit, which is said to take the form of a black pig haunting the grounds of Lydford Castle. Here his soul is doomed to spend the afterlife at the scene of similar brutality. For, although Jeffries never visited the location, the castle had formerly played a barbaric role in enforcing the harsh regime of Dartmoor tinners with swift punishment dispensed to all transgressors of forest laws. The last execution at Lydford Castle was carried out forty years before the Monmouth Rebellion during the Civil War when Tavistock poet William Browne wrote of the horrors that occurred in the name of justice which seem to sum up the philosophy of Judge Jeffries:

I have often heard of Lydford law
How in the morn they hang and draw
And sit in judgement after

Although Charles II once declared that Jeffries had 'no learning, no sense, no manners, and more impudence than ten carted streetwalkers', the judge was richly rewarded by James II for making examples of the yeomen from the 'nursery of rebellion' and elevated to the coveted position of Lord Chancellor which was commemorated in verse:

Well did thy wisely pruning hand
Lop off those suckers of the western land
That once designed to draw away
The vital sap of Britain's royal tree,
Whose prosp'rous strength's the only stay
Of Government, religion, equity
'Gainst rebel winds and storms they shall endure
And an adorned oak of trophies, last
Till Jeffries' fame's asleep and time itself be past

Unfortunately for Jeffries, the 'rebel winds and storms' were still blowing strongly in the West and three years later, an army led by William of Orange was welcomed at Brixham and succeeded where the Duke of Monmouth had failed. The judge was apprehended trying to flee the country disguised as a sailor. Westcountrymen would doubtless have seen it as 'poetic' justice if Jeffries had been hung, drawn and quartered like his hapless victims but he fell ill and died whilst a prisoner in the Tower of London. Curiously, the judge's father had tried to persuade his son to enter a quiet and respectable trade as he had experienced a premonition that a career in law would lead to an untimely end!

WILLIAM OF ORANGE & QUEEN MARY II

The Protestant Wind of Change

William, Prince of Orange (1650-1702) landed at Brixham in November 1688 at the invitation of English nobles who pleaded with him to overthrow King James II, a staunch Catholic who was trying to impose his beliefs on all of his subjects. The protestant son of William II of Orange and Mary, the daughter of Charles I of England, William also had the crucial support of his wife Princess Mary (1662-1694). For, she was the daughter of the monarch they planned to depose. Upon hearing the news that William and Mary had accepted the crown as joint sovereigns, King James pronounced a solemn curse on Mary for her treachery.

As the invasion fleet sailed into Torbay, local people swarmed to the coastline and cheered when they recognised the standard of the Prince raised on his ship named for his wife *Princess Mary*. According to tradition, William was rowed ashore at Brixham and stood up in the boat and announced in halting English, which fortunately for him was not misinterpreted: 'Mine good people, I am come for your goods. I am come for all your goods'. To which Mr Youlden replied on

A statue of William of Orange at Brixham Harbour.

behalf of the local populace: 'You'm welcome!' The prince then asked: 'Then if I am welcome, come and carry me ashore'. A strapping youth called Peter Varwell immediately waded in and William climbed onto his back. The stone where the future king first stepped ashore is now preserved in a monument on Brixham Quay.

Unsure of the reception he would receive elsewhere in his avowed intent to 'deliver the nation from popery'; William led his army inland and was greeted by Sir Edward Seymour of Berry Pomeroy. Remembering the fate of those who had appeared before Judge Jeffries after participating in the failure of the Monmouth Rebellion, many nobles were reluctant to affirm their allegiance, but Seymour, recently deposed as Recorder of Totnes by James II, had no such qualms. It is said that he provided the prince with a farmhouse at Longcombe, near Stoke Gabriel in which to hold his first 'parliament'. When introduced to his host, William enquired, 'I think, Sir Edward, that you are of the family of the Duke of Somerset'. Seymour politely corrected his guest, 'Pardon me, your Highness, the Duke of Somerset is one of my family'.

King James II.

When the army reached Newton Abbot, a proclamation on behalf of William – 'Glorious Defender of the Liberties of England' – was read out in the crowded market town, an event which is now commemorated in stone alongside the ancient tower of St Leonard's church where the bells pealed out a joyous welcome. Lord of the Manor, Sir William Courtenay absented himself, not wishing to compromise his position with King James, but left Forde House at the disposal of the prince who accepted the invitation to stay at the mansion where loud footsteps are attributed to his continuing ghostly presence. They are to be heard passing hurriedly down the corridors and doors fly open as the invisible spirit enters rooms. At the beginning of a perilous venture to wrest the crown of England from his father-in-law, William must have suffered extreme anxiety in this house and his hopes and fears for the future doubtless made him restless causing him to tramp restlessly up and down as he thought of the troubles ahead.

William's welcome in Devon proved to be a good omen. James II raised an army to intercept the invaders but was deserted by his generals and fled the country. The triumphant march to London was achieved without bloodshed to accomplish 'The Glorious Revolution'. The prince was drawn to England as the first stage of his designs on Europe. He never had the slightest love for England, using it as a treasure chest to further the interests of the Netherlands and fund their wars in Europe. The monarch became deeply unpopular and incurred huge debts, which led to the creation of the Bank of England that allowed Parliament to borrow vast amounts to subsidise the Nine Years War against France. Perhaps there is an element of justice that following William's death, caused by injuries sustained when a horse threw him, his spirit is

The Prince of Orange landing in Torbay.

condemned to haunt the country from which he absented himself at every possible opportunity during his reign.

Queen Mary had died of smallpox six years earlier. During her short reign she had capably assumed the responsibilities of head of state whilst the king was constantly away waging war. Although William was not the most companionable or faithful of husbands, Mary remained loyal to her husband and her protestant faith even when her father raised an army in Ireland in a doomed attempt to regain the crown. Like William, the spirit of Mary also visits South Devon. For, despite the fact that William was prepared for battle, leaving Mary safely behind in the Netherlands, a colourful legend persists. The local version of events claims that the Dutch invasion fleet had been blown slightly off course. Bad weather caused them to abandon their original intention to land at Dartmouth where Mary had arrived a week earlier and was anxiously waiting for her husband. Staying at what is now the Royal Castle Hotel, a messenger arrived at 2am to inform her of the prince's safe arrival, closely followed by a coach to transport Mary and her servants to Brixham. On each anniversary of this occasion a galloping horseman and a spectral coach re-enact this event. The clatter of hooves and the rumble of wheels on the phantom cobbles have awaked staff and guests in the early hours of the morning. Doors are opened and slammed shut before the royal princess embarks once more on her frantic journey to reach Brixham. Amongst her many attributes, Mary must also have been clairvoyant, for when the invasion force set sail, they actually steered a course towards South East England, before a 'protestant wind' brought about an enforced change of plan!

FLETCHER CHRISTIAN

Mutiny on the Bounty

The tyrannical sea captain William Bligh set out on his ill-fated voyage on HMS *Bounty* in 1788 to collect breadfruit plants from the Pacific Islands of Tahiti for transplanting in the West Indies. An idyllic life, basking in the tropical sun and fraternising with friendly native girls, unsettled the crew who were naturally reluctant to return to the harsh rigors of life at

Fletcher Christian and the mutineers look on as Captain Bligh and his supporters are cast adrift from the *Bounty*.

sea after their relaxing six month sojourn on the island. Also, Bligh's unpredictable temper led to personal clashes with his second-in-command Fletcher Christian (1764-1794), who complained that he had been 'treated like a dog all the voyage'. The result was an impulsive decision to seize the ship during the historic 'Mutiny on the Bounty'.

On 28 April 1789, Christian assumed command in a bloodless coup and cast Bligh, together with eighteen loyal followers, adrift in a heavily laden lifeboat. The irascible Devonian, who would be forever mocked, out of earshot of course, as 'Breadfruit Bligh', then proved his worth as a navigator. As befits a man who had served on a pioneering voyage to Australia under Captain Cook, he embarked on an epic journey of survival. Aboard a frail craft, equipped with only a compass and short on rations, the party covered 4,000 miles in six weeks, with the loss of only one life before reaching safety at Timor, East of Java.

The mutineers meanwhile, had split into two parties, the majority returned to the paradise of Tahiti, whilst Christian, realising that the Royal Navy would return to hunt them down, sailed off with eight other seamen aboard the *Bounty* to an unknown destination. In March 1791, HMS *Pandora*, under the command of Captain Edwards apprehended fourteen of the mutineers on Tahiti and clapped them in irons. The prisoners were held in a cage built on the quarterdeck. Disaster struck the *Pandora* when it struck a reef passing through the Endeavour Straits. As the sinking ship was abandoned, no order was given to release the prisoners, but a master of arms

Pitcairn Island.

sympathetically dropped his keys through the bars of the cage, allowing a few to escape drowning. Amongst the four survivors was a young midshipman, Peter Heywood, who had not participated in the mutiny, but had been compelled to remain on the *Bounty,* as there was no room in the open boat with Bligh's party. Treated savagely by the shipwrecked officers, eventual rescue brought another ordeal when the prisoners returned to England to face a court martial beginning on 12 September 1792. Following a six-day trial, sentence of death was passed on them all, with a recommendation of leniency for Heywood, who was later granted a full pardon and allowed to resume a successful career in the Royal Navy.

There was no further news of Christian until a remarkable encounter experienced by Peter Heywood in 1808. Late one evening, Heywood, now commanding his own vessel, was ashore in Devonport walking down Fore Street, when a man he immediately recognised as the leader of the mutiny passed him. Quickly turning and calling out Christian's name, he followed him around a corner to discover that his quarry had completely vanished. A thorough search of the area failed to find Christian and it was assumed he had returned to England and eluded the authorities.

However, the story took an amazing twist when, that same year, the master of an American merchantman landed at Pitcairn Island and discovered mutineer John Adams who claimed to be the sole survivor of Christian's party. For, according to Adams, the group had landed on the island in 1790 with their Tahitian wives and a dozen native male servants. After salvaging what they could from the *Bounty*, the ship was deliberately destroyed by fire to escape the attention of naval patrols with orders to capture the fugitives. Having spent a period of four years on the island, bitter disagreements broke out in the community and one night the Tahitian men attacked and murdered all the Englishmen bar Adams who was severely wounded. The women then extracted revenge for their husband's deaths by killing all their own countrymen whilst they were sleeping, leaving Adams as the only man on the island with nine women and numerous children fathered by himself and his fellow mutineers.

This being the case, Heywood could not have seen his former shipmate in Plymouth as Adams's story confirmed that Christian had then been dead for some fourteen years! Indeed,

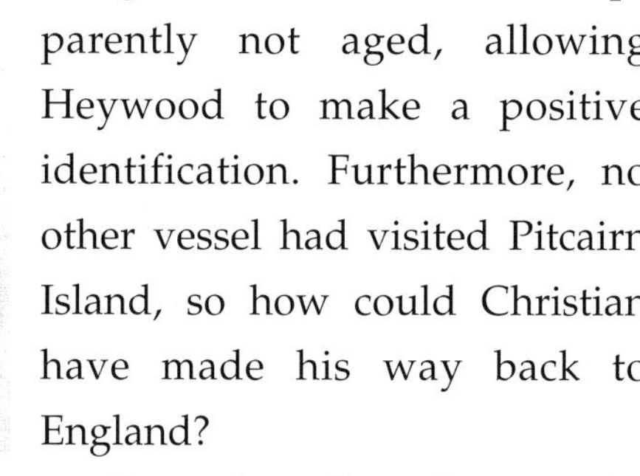
John Adams.

the sighting in Plymouth had taken place almost twenty years after the mutiny; therefore, it was strange that the figure of Christian had apparently not aged, allowing Heywood to make a positive identification. Furthermore, no other vessel had visited Pitcairn Island, so how could Christian have made his way back to England?

Coincidentally, during the year 1808, Fletcher's old tormentor, William Bligh faced another mutiny in his capacity as Governor of New South Wales. His highhanded treatment of the military commander resulted in troops marching on Government House and placing him under house arrest for nearly a year, before he was released and exiled to Tasmania. Perhaps, whilst this drama was being played out the jubilant spirit of Fletcher Christian had returned to haunt the streets of Plymouth – the city of William Bligh's birth!

NAPOLEON BONAPARTE

The Little General of Berry Head

The Battle of Waterloo finally brought peace to Europe, which had suffered over twenty years of warfare, inflicted by the 'Disturber of the World' – Napoleon Bonaparte (1769-1821). The self-crowned Emperor of France had been forced to abdicate in 1814, but executed a daring escape from exile on the isle of Elba before his bid to regain power ended in a crushing defeat at the hands of the Duke of Wellington. Fleeing from the battlefield, 'Boney' found he was unwelcome in France, where the monarchy had been restored and Louis XVIII had branded him a 'rebel and traitor'. His plan to reach the sanctuary of America was foiled by a naval blockade; therefore, he somewhat optimistically applied to live amongst the enemy and instantly became Britain's most celebrated asylum seeker.

With an entourage of fifty close followers and servants, Napoleon gave himself up to the Royal Navy. On mounting the deck of the man 'o' war HMS *Bellerophon*, Napoleon politely introduced himself to the ship's commander Captain Maitland, 'Sir, I come to claim the protection of your king and your laws'. The party sailed from France to Torbay where the Channel Fleet had been stationed and a strategic garrison assembled at

Berry Head during the Napoleonic Wars to repel an intended invasion, which never materialised. The *Bellerophon* anchored off the Orestone on 24 July 1815 whilst the British Government considered the shock request of their distinguished 'guest'.

Napoleon was an instant tourist attraction and seeing there was money to be made, one enterprising entrepreneur cheekily offered to take the French celebrity off the navy's hands and exhibit him in a cage. Bonaparte had dismissed Britain as 'a nation of shopkeepers' but was now inadvertently benefiting such traders when sightseers from all over the country flocked to Devon. Hordes of people tried to catch a glimpse of the great man from a flotilla of small craft, which put out to sea from Torquay, Paignton, Brixham, Teignmouth, Dawlish, Exeter and Sidmouth. The fallen emperor spent long periods pacing the deck and when he went below, Jolly Jack Tars helpfully informed the public of his whereabouts by chalking up signs on a board, 'He's gone to dine' – 'Writing with his officers' – 'Coming upon deck'. If boats tried to draw alongside the *Bellerophon*, however, the sailors amused themselves by playfully dousing the unsuspecting occupants below with buckets of water.

At his first sight of the South Devon coastline Napoleon exclaimed, 'What a beautiful country!' However, he was not allowed to go ashore and no visitors were allowed to board and pay their respects. This included the local gentry who had to content themselves with sending gifts of fruit and flowers to the ship. Although labelled 'the most infamous of criminals' there was considerable admiration for Napoleon, which turned

Napoleon on the *Bellerophon*.

to sympathy when it was announced that he was to be banished to the inhospitable island of St Helena. Sections of the British press argued strongly that this move was illegal without a trial. Furthermore, as hostilities had ceased and Napoleon was no longer a head of state, they believed he was entitled to be released just like any common prisoner of war.

Bellerophon sailed to Plymouth to transfer the prisoner to HMS *Northumberland*, which would transport the party to its destination in the South Atlantic. Once again thousands of curiosity seekers besieged the ship and one boat was accidentally mown down in The Sound by a naval vessel, causing the death of a stone mason from Devonport Dockyard. With safety in mind, the *Bellerophon* immediately withdrew back to Berry Head but this did not avoid a similar tragedy, which resulted in the drowning of two ladies as the prisoner was being prepared for deportation on Monday 7 August. On board the *Bellerophon*, Madame Bertrand, the wife of Napoleon's closest confidante was overcome with grief at the thought of being parted from her sovereign and was only saved from suicide by a quick thinking officer who clung on to her as she attempted to throw herself out of a port-hole.

Napoleon was suffering from a bilious complaint, but his personal physician declined to accompany him to St Helena and a ship's doctor from the Royal Navy volunteered to take his place. However, the journey into exile with four friends and twelve servants left 'Boney' a broken man and he lost the will to live.

When informed by a courtier that 'your greatest enemy is dead', King George IV was ecstatic before realising that the news concerned Napoleon, not the demise of his estranged wife Queen Caroline. On the day of the deposed emperor's death, a curious incident occurred at Berry Head Fort. An alert sentry from the Devon Militia spotted someone approaching and called out, 'Who goes there?' An eerie silence met his challenge and the mysterious stranger began fading into the mist. Suddenly, the stunned soldier recognised the unmistakeable figure of the 'Little General' wearing his trademark cocked hat and striking a typical pose with his right arm tucked inside his tunic. It appears that the spirit of Napoleon took the earliest opportunity to set foot in the country he had failed to conquer, choosing the last spot he had glimpsed before his banishment to certain death!

BISHOP HENRY PHILLPOTTS

The Bishop's Walk

From the moment he was offered the Bishopric of Exeter in 1830, controversy embroiled the life of Henry Phillpotts (1778-1869). Whilst the move to Devon represented a significant promotion from his previous position as the Dean of Chester, he insisted that with a wife and eighteen children to support, he could not afford to accept the appointment unless he was allowed to retain a lucrative secondary post as Rector of Stanhope-on-the-Wear. When granted permission for this arrangement, Phillpotts' parishioners in Durham petitioned against the decision, complaining bitterly that he was lining his pockets whilst delegating his duties to a 'hireling'. Such financial arrangements were not unusual at the time, although Phillpotts took a hypocritical stance against local clergy who did likewise.

Many of the more affluent of them lived abroad and never went anywhere near their 'livings' in Devon. The bishop refused to tolerate this lax attitude and declared war on his absentee clerics demanding 'Reside or Resign!'

'Henry of Exeter' did little to endear himself to the people of that city. Within months of his consecration, angry protestors assailed the Episcopal palace after he had voted against the Reform Bill. The bishop had used his newly acquired influence in the House of Lords to speak out strongly against proposed legislation, which would extend the franchise and increase the electorate by 50% in England and Wales. An ugly situation was only averted when his son summoned guards to disperse the mob. When a cholera epidemic struck the population in 1832, Phillpotts committed a public relations disaster by abandoning his flock in Exeter and fleeing out of harm's way to the safety of Torquay. Here he settled permanently and built a palatial villa in the Italianate style called Bishopstowe, situated close to Anstey's Cove and a cliff path which became known as the 'Bishop's Walk'.

Bishop Henry Phillpotts.

The bishop enjoyed a formidable reputation as a strict high churchman and enforced absolute ecclesiastical correctness on his clergy. The placing of flowers upon the altar particularly annoyed him. On Easter Day 1847, he visited St John's church,

Torquay and noticed a floral cross and two vases of flowers adorning the altar, which he furiously knocked off with a stick. Furthermore, the culprit, the Reverend Parks Smith was hauled before a court of inquiry at Exeter, admonished and ordered to pay costs. Ever after he had to endure the cruel nickname 'Flowerpot Smith'. The foxhunting patron of the rector at Haccombe, Sir Walter Carew, enjoyed being the scourge of the bishop, for due to a medieval edict; the parish was the direct responsibility of the Archbishop of Canterbury. Making the most of this unique ecclesiastical freedom, Carew threatened to set his hounds on the bishop's luckless Rural Dean when he approached Haccombe. Phillpotts soon had his revenge by reporting the Rector of Haccombe to his archbishop for aiding and abetting the patron of the living in refusing to allow the Rural Dean from performing his rightful duties.

An unfortunate victim of the bishop's vindictive nature was the Reverend James Shore who in 1846 was accused of conducting services in an unlicensed building at Bridgetown, Totnes. Tried before the Court of Arches, the case was proved and he was flung into a debtors prison until a public appeal enabled him to pay costs. Totnes MP, Lord Seymour, launched an attack on the bishop's handling of the case, which was supported by journalist Thomas Latimer in an inflammatory editorial in the *Western Times*: 'Everlastingly in hot water, but never clean withal... he [Phillpotts] stands branded as a consecrated, careless perverter of facts, and one who does no credit to the mitre...' Phillpotts took legal action against Latimer for libel and defamation, which was heard, at Exeter

Castle. The judge in his summing up made it quite clear to the grand jury that his sympathies lay with Phillpotts; however, they took great pleasure in ignoring his directive and found for the defendant. Cheers greeted the verdict and Phillpotts learned just how unpopular he was as church bells were rung in celebration of his defeat at Newton Abbot, Ashburton, Moretonhamstead, Bideford, South Molton and Barnstaple.

Bishop Phillpotts survived his wife by six years and was buried beside her at St Marychurch parish church. Bishopstowe was demolished in 1921, although part of the old house was incorporated into a new building, the Palace Hotel. On the bicentenary of his birth in 1978, the *Herald Express* reported that the ghost of Bishop Phillpotts had often been spotted strolling along the lobbies of the hotel and could be the answer to a staff shortage: 'If I could catch him I would have a uniform on him straight away and put him in the dining room' quipped the manager. One member of staff confirmed that the claims about the bishop walking in the hotel were true: 'I have seen him myself' said the deputy head porter, 'I have no doubt that he exists. He was standing in front of me, and as I walked towards him he just melted away. As soon as I saw him, I felt terribly cold'.

CHARLES KINGSLEY

The Beachcomber of Westward Ho!

Best remembered as a children's writer of classic tales *The Water Babies, Hereward the Wake* and *Westward Ho!* churchman, social reformer, marine biologist, artist, essayist, poet and novelist Charles Kingsley (1819-75) was born on the edge of Dartmoor at Holne vicarage where his father, Charles senior, was curate. His mother Mary loved Devon so much that she constantly walked about the countryside during her pregnancy, hoping to communicate the passion to her unborn child.

The family moved to a number of parishes around the country before accepting the living of Clovelly in North Devon from 1830-36. Two years later, son Charles entered Cambridge University where he was awarded a first class degree in the classics before he was ordained to the curacy of Eversley in Hampshire. Married to Fanny in 1844, his wife became seriously ill ten years later and his bishop granted him six months leave of absence for a period of convalescence in Devon. Taking up residence in Torquay, Kingsley's radical views supporting Chartist social reform led to him being banned from accepting lucrative invitations to give sermons in local churches by the tyrannical Bishop of Exeter, Henry Phillpotts, whose ecclesiastical palace Bishopstowe was located in the resort. Shrugging off this rebuke, Kingsley turned his attention to marine biology. Accompanied by acknowledged expert Phillip Gosse, the curate spent his days wandering along the beaches at low tide, searching for specimens of sea life, pouring over them at night with magnifying glass and scalpel and producing exquisite drawings and water colours which led to the publication of his explorations and discoveries in the book *Glaucus* or *Wonders of the Shore.*

While residing on the shore at Livermead House, a short distance from Torre Abbey, where Francis Drake had ordered the detention of 400 prisoners of war captured when his fire ships put flight to the Spanish Armada, Kingsley developed the germ of an idea for a historical novel. He set out his thoughts in a letter to a friend:

> Torbay is a place which endears itself to patriot, the naturalist and the artist. We cannot gaze on its blue ring of water and limestone buffs which bound it to the north and south without a glow passing through our hearts as we remember the terrible and glorious pageant which passed by it in the bright days of July 1588, when the Spanish Armada ventured slowly past Berry Head with Elizabeth's gallant pack of Devon's captains following fast in its wake ...

Charles Kingsley.

Taking this historical theme, the author located the story in his native North Devon; the result was *Westward Ho!* a swashbuckling tale of derring-do, featuring heroic Devonshire seaman Amyas Leigh and his escapades during the threat of invasion by the Spaniards. Published in 1855 to great acclaim, it also served as a reminder of past glories to feed the nation's patriotic fervour at the height of the Crimean War. The best-selling novel was completed by the author while staying at Northdown Hall in Bideford. From here, he often journeyed along the coast to Northam Burrows with its Pebble Ridge on a sandy beach stretching for over two miles that would become part of a popular holiday destination when it was developed into the only place-name in England with an exclamation mark – Westward Ho! Kingsley resolutely refused to give his blessing to the resort named in honour of his novel. Furthermore, he could scarcely disguise his abhorrence of the project. His attitude about the development of tourism was summed up in a letter written in 1864:

> How goes on the Northam Burrows scheme for spoiling that beautiful place with hotels and villas. I suppose it must be, but you will frighten away all the sea-pies [oyster catchers] and defile the Pebble Ridge with chicken bones and sandwich scraps.

In his introduction to *Glaucus*, Kingsley described holidaymakers as that 'ignoble army of idlers who saunter about the sands and cliffs and quays'. Conversely, his glorious descriptions of the area in *Westward Ho!* inevitably attracted the attention of the very people he derided:

> All who have travelled through the delicious scenery of North Devon must needs know the Little White Town of Bideford which slopes upwards from its broad tide river paved with yellow sand and many old arched bridge where salmon wait for autumn floods, towards the pleasant upland on the west.

Although, he steadfastly avoided visiting the new resort in his lifetime, shortly after his death, his tranquil spirit was spotted at his favourite 'haunt' – wandering along the shore where he used to employ quarrymen to move large boulders so that he could take time to examine the marine life on his beloved Pebble Ridge.

RUDYARD KIPLING

The Brooding Spirit of Rock House

The Nobel Prize for Literature, introduced in 1901, was not awarded to an English language writer until December 1907, when Rudyard Kipling (1865-1936) became its youngest recipient 'in consideration of the power of observation, originality of imagination, virility of ideas and remarkable talent for narration which characterize the creations of this world-famous author'.

The creator of literary classics including the *Jungle Book* and the *Just So* stories was born in India and named after Lake Rudyard in Staffordshire where his parents had first met. At the age of six, he and his three-year old sister Trix were brought to England

Rudyard Kipling.

and deposited, without any explanation by their parents, at a boarding house in Southsea. Here they were raised and educated by a retired naval officer and his wife until 1878 when Rudyard entered the United Services College at Westward Ho! Founded four years earlier, ostensibly to prepare boys for a military or naval career, this was never the intention for Kipling, as the college was chosen solely because his mother was a close friend of the headmaster Cormwell Price. Despite a miserable initiation period at the school, which he later recalled was 'primitive in its appointments, and our food would now raise a mutiny in Dartmoor [Prison]', the budding author flourished when the head realised 'I was irretrievably committed to the ink-pot', Rudyard was appointed editor of the school magazine. A collection of his poems written at the college was published in India by his parents who believed in his potential. With fond memories of the establishment dubbed by Kipling as 'the school before its time' he joyously returned to his family and embarked upon a journalistic career. He also drew inspiration from the land of his birth for his early literary successes. His output was stupendous and he became a marvellous storyteller standing by the maxim that 'A word – should fall in its place like a bell in a full chime'.

After travelling extensively, Kipling married American Caroline Baleister in 1892. The couple settled in her hometown of Brattleboro, Vermont, but their happiness was destroyed when Rudyard quarrelled with his brother-in-law whom he had arrested for making violent threats – resulting in an embarrassing court appearance and damaging publicity. In the autumn of 1896, the Kiplings left this bitter episode behind them and moved to England. They rented Rock House at Maidencombe, Torquay, built on a cliff overlooking a small cove. The author described the villa as 'almost too good to be true' and waxed lyrical about the location, 'I look straight from my work table on to the decks of the fishing craft who come in to look after their lobster pots'. With the publication of his latest work *The Seven Seas*, Kipling proudly accepted an invitation to spend several days with the naval cadets based on the training ship *Britannia* at Dartmouth.

Kipling's enthusiasm for his new home declined as a sense of evil and brooding depression enveloped the household, which would later inspire his ghost story *The House Surgeon*. He revealed a gathering blackness of mind and sorrow of the heart, 'It was the Feng-shui – the Spirit of the house itself – that darkened the sunshine and fell upon us every time we entered, checking the very words on our lips'. He also disapproved of the posturing wealthy residents of the town. 'Torquay is such a place that I do desire acutely to upset by dancing through with nothing on but my spectacles'. For a time, he tried to fit in and took up the current craze for cycling. The gossip columnist of a local paper reported 'I saw Mr. Rudyard Kipling careering along the Tor Abbey sands on wheels one day last week'. The hobby ended when he and his wife shared pedalling duties on 'a tandem bicycle, whose double steering-bars made good dependence for continuous domestic quarrel'. The couple crashed off their 'devil's toast rack' and walked home pushing the bike they dubbed 'Hell Spider'.

Before his brief sojourn on the English Riviera came to an abrupt end, Kipling fictionalised his schooldays. Local author Eden Phillpotts, best remembered for a cycle of eighteen novels set on Dartmoor, sent a copy of his latest book to Kipling, which immediately triggered an idea. Early in 1897, Kipling broached the subject with his editor: 'The notion of writing a Devonshire tale is new to me but, now I come to think of it, I was educated at Westward Ho! nigh Bideford and for six puppy years [four in fact] talked vernacular with the natives whose apples I stole. What will E.P. give to buy me off?' The result was *Stalky & Co.* based on the adventures of himself and his two closest friends at United Services College. His former headmaster Cormwell Price spent some time in Torquay hearing passages from the new book read to him by the excited author. Another rare happy moment occurred at Rock House when Caroline learned she was expecting the couple's third child. The Kiplings immediately executed 'our flight from Torquay' in May 1897 and sought refuge with relatives near Brighton. John Kipling, the son conceived in Torquay was doomed to die in action during the First World War. His father had to live with the guilt of his son's fate after 'pulling strings' to arrange for his enlistment after he had been rejected on medical grounds with extremely poor eyesight. Little wonder that when Rudyard revisited his former home shortly before his own death, the writer detected 'the same brooding Spirit of deep, deep Despondency within the open lit rooms'.

ISAMBARD KINGDOM BRUNEL

The Little Giant of St Marychurch

The greatest engineer of the Industrial Revolution, Isambard Kingdom Brunel (1806-1859) designed and built some of the world's finest viaducts, bridges, tunnels, ships and railways. Amongst his outstanding achievements was the pioneering iron-built boat The Great Western – the first steamship to cross the Atlantic, the architectural splendour of Paddington Railway Station and the elegant Clifton Suspension Bridge spanning the Avon Gorge at Bristol. The charismatic innovator also left his mark in Devon with the bold experiment of the Atmospheric Engine, the completion of the scenic railroad running along the beautiful coastline of South Devon's holiday resorts and the construction of the Royal Albert Bridge at Saltash, enabling trains to cross the River Tamar.

At the age of twenty-six, Brunel was appointed chief engineer to the newly formed Great Western Railway. By the time he had supervised the construction of the London to Bristol line that opened in 1841, the GWR was well on its way to becoming known as 'God's Wonderful Railway' by steam enthusiasts. After extending the line from Bristol to Exeter, Brunel undertook the building of the South Devon Railway from Exeter to Torquay. For this venture, he attempted to introduce a revolutionary new system – the Atmospheric Engine. Instead of trains being pulled by locomotives, they were propelled by air pressure. Stationary engines, housed in Pumping Stations, were placed every 5 kilometres along the track at Exeter, Starcross, Dawlish, Teignmouth, Newton Abbot, Torquay and Totnes. To operate the system, air was sucked along a pipe laid between the tracks that moved the train forward when linked to the leading carriage. Trials took place between Exeter and Teignmouth but ended in a rare failure for Brunel. Running costs escalated when rats found the leather valves coated in grease extremely appetising and the damage they caused resulted in loss of air pressure. Interminable delays to progress resulted in the scheme's financial backers losing confidence in the project that was eventually abandoned in favour of a conventional railroad – albeit running on Brunel's broad gauge tracks, which would also be standardised in 1892.

Brunel had a strong urge to settle in South Devon. It became a forlorn hope of his to escape the overwhelming pressures of work and retire to the county that meant so much to him, as his mother Sophia Kingdom had been born and raised in Plymouth. During the last ten years of his life, he spent the summers with his family staying in a rented villa at Torquay. He purchased 163 acres of land on the outskirts of the town at Watcombe Park, in the parish of St Marychurch, which he

Isambard Kingdom Brunel.

described as 'an estate where all is to be done'. Brunel supervised the building of new roads, planted the bare hillsides with trees and laid out the grounds advised by landscape gardener William Nesfield. The foremost country-house architect of the day, William Burn, was commissioned to draw up plans for a mansion and the foundations were laid but sadly, Brunel did not live to see dream home completed. A fatal kidney disease was diagnosed and the great man passed away in his prime. His son, Isambard testified about his father's love for Watcombe, for it was here 'that the happiest hours of his life were spent'.

Brunel and his wife Mary had generously supported worthy causes and involved themselves in local affairs. She founded a school at Barton and in 1854 he successfully spoke out on behalf of the neighbourhood to the House of Lords who agreed to his objections and threw out a ludicrous proposal to spoil the beauty of Babbacombe Beach by siting a Gas Works

St Marychurch parish church.

there. Regularly attending St Marychurch parish church, Brunel was the largest single contributor to rebuilding work and also made a generous donation to provide a new church organ. Soon after his death, brought about by sheer exhaustion and overwork after packing an enormous amount of activity into his short life, there were reported sightings on the streets of Babbacombe and St Marychurch of a small ghostly figure wearing the innovative engineer's trademark 'stovepipe' hat. Furthermore, a local character in an intoxicated state was walking past the parish church on his way home from the pub one night, when he spotted the ghost of 'The Little Giant'. The apparition walked up the path towards the church and passed through the closed wooden doors. This strange occurrence was followed by the strains of ethereal music coming from the church organ in the empty church. Running away as fast as his unsteady legs could carry him, the drunk quickly sobered up due to the shock of this terrifying experience. Despite the incredulous reception by his friends to his wild tale, he took the pledge and it was said that he was never tempted to touch another drop as long as he lived!

JOHN LEE

The Pub Sign They Could Not Hang

Despite his pleas of innocence, young manservant John Lee (1864-1945) was convicted in 1885 of the gruesome murder of his elderly female employer, Emma Keyse, at her seaside home on Babbacombe Beach. Incredibly, he escaped hanging when the trapdoors of the scaffold at Exeter Prison inexplicably failed to open on three occasions. The death penalty was commuted to life imprisonment and upon his release twenty-two years later in December 1907; he married and cashed in on his notoriety by making personal appearances in public houses. During such an engagement in London he eloped with a barmaid abandoning his wife who was expecting their second child. He then seemingly disappeared without trace and it was only recently discovered that he died in 1945 when his grave was located in Milwaukee, America, further fuelling the legend surrounding 'The Man They Could Not Hang'.

A strange event added to the mystery over a century later when a pub named the John Lee opened on Babbacombe Downs at Easter 1989. At the beginning of June, the swinging pub sign bearing the logo of a hanged man, fell to the ground on three consecutive nights for no discernible reason. That same week, Steve Harley and his band Cockney Rebel were appearing in concert in Exeter. It had just been announced that the talented singer-songwriter was to play the role of John Lee in a forthcoming movie and on the B-side of his latest single he had recorded the self-composed theme tune *Babbacombe Lee* Surprisingly, in view of the world-wide interest in the case, the only previous movie of the story was an Australian silent film loosely based on John Lee's best-selling autobiography *The*

Discovering the Babbacombe Murder.

Man They Could Not Hang published in 1908. The film proved so successful that extra scenes were added before the film was introduced to Britain. When shown at the Empire Cinema, Newton Abbot, in May 1925, members of Lee's family sat amongst the packed houses. For the British attempt, a tiny bay just outside Brixham was selected for the setting of the film, where a mock Victorian villa was to be built to re-create the scene of the murder (Emma Keyse's home The Glen had been demolished in 1894). Extensive and dedicated research by the filmmakers had reportedly uncovered new facts about the murder and been incorporated into the script which had two possible endings. The producer told the press: 'I've lived and breathed this for so long now that I'm not going to give up until I have discovered the truth'. Unfortunately, the 'truth' never came out as the film was suddenly abandoned, soon followed by the closure of the Babbacombe pub. Perhaps the two projects had earned the displeasure of John Lee's troubled spirit!

At the time of John Lee's deliverance, when he became the only man in British legal history to survive the method of execution known as the 'long drop', there was speculation that he had been saved by either an act of God or the work of the Devil. In stark contrast to the prosecution's portrayal of a depraved lunatic capable of smashing an old lady's head with an axe, then slashing her throat with a knife before setting fire to the lifeless body, the judge in passing sentence of death remarked how calm the demeanour of the accused had been throughout the trial, to which John Lee leaned forward in the

The Man They Could Not Hang.

dock and replied firmly: 'The reason why I am so calm is that I trust in the Lord, and He knows I am innocent'. In the days leading up to the date of execution, Lee read the Bible prodigiously and intimated to the prison chaplain that the real culprit was the lover of his half-sister, Elizabeth Harris, who was cook at The Glen and expecting a child which was later delivered out of wedlock in Newton Abbot Workhouse. Following his reprieve, Lee announced his belief that he had been saved by divine intervention and on the morning of the execution, told two prison guards that he had dreamt that 'Three times the bolt was drawn, and three times the bolt failed to act'. As Lee predicted between each of the three attempts, the trapdoors were tested and opened normally, but refused to budge as soon as he stood upon them. It was also rumoured that throughout the ordeal on the scaffold, a white dove perched on the gallows until the condemned man was led safely back to his prison cell.

Contradicting this view, friends of Lee claimed they had paid a white witch handsomely to save him from the noose. Country folk told stories of how John Lee's mother had visited the church graveyard near her home at Abbotskerswell, recited the Lord's Prayer backwards and summoned the Evil One to save her son, whilst Granny Lee of Ogwell told locals: 'They shall not hang him' as she walked to Exeter on the morning of the execution and cast a spell on the gallows from a spot overlooking the prison. In 1905, the witchcraft theory gained credence from a surprising source – the Archdeacon of Westminster, Basil Wilberforce. At the time of the murder he had been a regular visitor to Babbacombe where he addressed temperance meetings organised by a distinguished neighbour

John 'Babbacombe' Lee.

of Emma Keyse, Lady Mount-Temple of Babbacombe Cliff. The churchman was chaplain to the House of Commons and vehemently opposed a growing campaign for Lee's release informing the Home Office that he 'knew the Lees well' and they were 'a well known witch family on Dartmoor'.

Miracle or sorcery, the events on the scaffold cast doubt in many people's minds about Lee's guilt, much to the dismay of the editor of the *Times* who poured scorn on the Home Secretary's decision to reprieve Lee believing that his action would, 'encourage foolish and superstitious people to believe, in spite of evidence as clear as noonday, that Lee was wrongfully convicted'.

OSCAR WILDE

Wilde About Torquay

Literary genius Oscar Wilde (1854-1900) was at the height of his fame in November 1892, when he arranged to stay in Torquay for a period of three months. He leased Babbacombe Cliff from the owner Lady Mount-Temple, a distant cousin and confidante of Oscar's wife Constance. Her mansion was designed by John Ruskin – Wilde's former lecturer on Florentine Art at Oxford University. William Morris who named all the bedrooms after flowers created the interior décor. Oscar worked in the most artistic room in the house 'Wonderland' which was agreeable to Oscar's aesthetic tastes, for adorning the walls were paintings by Pre-Raphaelite artists Burne-Jones and Rossetti. Wilde also relaxed by swimming and sailing with his two sons off Babbacombe Beach. He wrote to Lady Mount-Temple whilst she was wintering abroad: 'I find the peace and beauty here so good for troubled nerves, and so suggestive for new work'.

During his stay, Oscar completed the play *A Woman of No Importance* and made arrangements to publish a limited edition of *Salome*, which had been banned from the stage by the Lord Chancellor because it depicted Biblical characters. In February

Oscar Wilde.

1893, he sent a copy to distinguished literary critic and Torquay resident, Edmund Gosse: 'Accept it as a slight tribute of my admiration of your own delicate use of the English'. Earlier, Wilde had supervised rehearsals of an amateur production of *Lady Windermere's Fan* directed by the Mayoress, Mrs Splatt, which opened in January 1893 at Torquay's Theatre Royal. He also granted an interview to local history author and solicitor Percy Almy that appeared in the magazine *The Theatre*.

Amongst the topics they discussed were the merits of famous poets; Keats was the absolute 'favourite' of Wilde, Tennyson 'a supreme artist', Shelley 'a magnificent genius' though too 'ethereal'. Wilde had little regard for the work of Robert Browning, nor his wife Elizabeth, who before her marriage had spent three years recuperating from smallpox in Torquay. Almy observed that Wilde had 'an engaging charm' which would win him many disciples and interestingly, in view of the scandal that was about to engulf him, recorded the great man's thoughts on criminals, 'Never attempt to reform a man, men never repent'.

Early in February, Constance left to join friends in Florence. Immediately, Oscar was joined by his close friend Lord Alfred 'Bosie' Douglas, accompanied by his tutor who wrote of Wilde whilst staying in Babbacombe: 'I think him perfectly delightful with the firmest conviction that his morals are detestable'. Two years later, the relationship between Wilde and Bosie was to incite the boy's father the Marquess of Queensbury

The Marquess of Queensbury.

into denouncing Wilde as a 'sodomite'. Oscar responded by bringing an ill-advised libel case against Queensbury in April 1895. Produced in evidence was a damning letter written at Babbacombe Cliff, where Wilde had responded to a poem that Douglas had sent him: 'My boy, Your sonnet is quite lovely, and it is a marvel that those red rose-leaf lips of yours should have been made no less for music of song than for madness of kisses. Your slim gilt soul walks between passion and poetry. I know Hyacinthus, whom Apollo loved so madly, was you in Greek days'. His case collapsed and Oscar immediately found himself facing criminal charges on twenty-five acts of gross indecency allegedly committed with a number of youths.

Two trials were necessary to decide Oscar's fate when the jury failed to agree a verdict. During the first, Constance sought refuge from the press at Babbacombe Cliff with Lady Mount-Temple. Whilst there, she wrote a letter seeking guidance from a fortune teller, Mrs Robinson: 'What is to become of my husband who has so betrayed me and deceived me and ruined the lives of my darling boys?' The lady had already given the answer two years earlier at a party after the London opening of *A Woman of No* importance. Wilde was noticeably distressed when told that his right palm revealed that he would 'send himself into exile'. Indeed, after serving two years hard labour in Reading Gaol, Wilde fled to France, where in his own words he was soon 'dying beyond my means'. Loyal friends bore the cost of his funeral and one of them complained with unintended Wildean wit: 'Dying in Paris is really a very difficult and expensive luxury for a foreigner!'

During the centenary of Wilde's birth in 1954, the Torquay Operatic and Drama Society (TOADS) produced *A Woman of No Importance* at Babbacombe Theatre located alongside Babbacombe Cliff. During rehearsals the set designer saw who he presumed to be an actor in period costume walking towards him. Oddly, in his lapel was a sunflower, famously favoured by Wilde. When the bemused designer stared closely, the figure suddenly disappeared into thin air. From that day forward, members of the company experienced an 'eerie' feeling and were reluctant to enter a particular dressing room alone. When the TOADS relocated to the Little Theatre in the 1990s, it appears they did not escape the influence of the Irish wit. The production of *An Ideal Husband* was hit by crisis when the actor playing the lead role failed to turn up for the opening performance. With a full house waiting expectedly, the director stepped in to save the show – with no time for preparation he was forced to appear on stage reading his lines from Oscar's script!

BEATRICE CHASE & ABBOT BONIFACE NATTER

Heaven in Devon

Olive Katharine Parr (1874-1955) claimed to be directly descended from the brother of Catharine Parr, the sixth and last wife of King Henry VIII. Proud of her royal heritage, she sealed her letters and private papers with a signet engraved with the Rose of Lancaster. However, far from her ancestral northern roots she found fame and her spiritual home in Devon and adopting the pen-name Beatrice Chase was awarded a honorary title in a book dedicated to her by fellow novelist John Oxenham – *My Lady of the Moor*.

In 1895, Olive joined the Order of St Dominic and took the vow of chastity. As

Beatrice Chase.

a Dominican Tertiary she worked in the slums of East End London, became a prison visitor and was active in the Children's Crusade of Rescue, until her health failed. On doctor's advice her mother took her to recuperate at the seaside. Journeying to Dawlish in June 1901, a hotel guest was concerned about the invalid's serious condition and helpfully suggested 'Get her away to Dartmoor while there is still time'. Following this advice, Mrs Parr, a woman of independent means with an income from an estate in Lancashire, found rooms at Widecombe where the immediate improvement in her daughter's well-being seemed nothing short of miraculous. Beatrice later wrote that 'the moor saved my life and transformed me into a robust woman'.

Mother and daughter continued to spend spring and summer holidays at Widecombe, renting a thatched cottage, Venton House, which, they so loved, that they eventually purchased the property and moved to the area permanently. They let the adjoining land to tenants and converted a farmhouse into the St Michaels' Little Home of Rest for 'poor gentlewomen working in large cities'. In order to restore Catholic worship to the parish, they then obtained permission from the Bishop of Plymouth to build a chapel. Unable to fund the cost of the project, Beatrice sought the advice of Father Boniface Natter (1866-1906), who had been elected the first Abbot of Buckfastleigh since the Reformation when the community was granted abbey status in 1902. Dedicated to restoring the ruins of the 'Cathedral of Dartmoor', a testament of faith that was eventually realised in 1938, the abbot was tragically drowned in the wreck of the *Sirio* off the coast of Spain during a voyage to a mission in South America. With the loss of her chief supporter, Beatrice grew disheartened and recorded her feelings in a poem *My Heaven in Devon*:

Oh my friend, my friend, and is this the end
When our friendship had scarce begun?
My hopes have flown, I am left alone,
And the light has gone from the sun,
The light from my life and the sun.

For the sea so blue she has taken you
And has left not a trace behind;
Our sick hearts pine as we seek a sign,
A sign that we long to find,
That we seek and never shall find

Abbot Boniface Natter.

After months of fervent prayer, the answer to the problem came one evening at twilight as Beatrice was leaning on the garden gate. She suddenly became aware of the unmistakeable presence of the deceased abbot standing beside her. She could neither see nor hear anything, but was clearly conscious of an inner voice calmly reassuring her that she could afford to build an extension to her cottage that would grant her dearest wish:

For lo! A well loved presence was beside me,
As lone I lingered by the gate,
And then I knew no harm could e'er betide me,
For his clear answer held my blessed fate.

'Remain at Venton, where your heart's ambition
At little cost ere long shall be fulfilled:
Fear not, but ponder well my admonition:
Within these garden walls begin to build'.

Mrs Parr drew up the plans herself to save architects fees and when workmen began digging the foundations in January 1908, they made an amazing cost-cutting discovery, for just below the sods, they struck granite, 'hard as flint, white as marble and enough to build a chapel'.

Having established herself as a novelist whilst writing under her own name in London, family names were used for the pseudonym Beatrice Chase to produce her first Dartmoor book *The Heart of the Moor* that became a best-seller. Similar success was gained with shrewd observations of country life in her next title *From a Dartmoor Window*. Fame brought unwanted 'hordes of trippers' to Venton, and Beatrice hung forbidding notices on her property to keep her admiring

The Chapel at Venton.

readers at bay. Her behaviour became more eccentric following the death of her mother in 1926 and she gained a reputation for irritability and rudeness, as she gradually became a recluse, tended by a succession of retired seafarers whom she engaged as her servant and always referred to as 'Mr Bluejacket'.

When she lost a long battle with cancer at Newton Abbot Hospital, Beatrice was clothed in her Dominican Tertiary habit and buried in the churchyard at Widecombe. Four years later, a public appeal raised money for a gravestone made from granite in the shape of a Nun's Cross. On one side was carved 'Beatrice Chase 1874-1955' and on the other side 'Pray for me Olive Katherine Parr' However, in her will, the author had insisted that her last resting place should be alongside the graves of her pets in a field by her home, taking care to leave 'the three little cats undisturbed under the big stones at my feet'. Now her spirit remains restless in the hereafter, longing for her final wish to be granted and The Lady of the Moor's ghost roams the land that was her home for fifty years, seeking peace and sanctuary near Venton House.

VIOLET TWEEDALE & BEVERLEY NICHOLS

The Ghost Hunters of Castel a Mare

During the Victorian age, Torquay became a popular 'watering place', attracting wealthy patrons who leased palatial villas in the exclusive residential area of The Warberries. Unusually, one property stood derelict for decades and fell into ruin, giving rise to rumours that it was a haunted house. Early in the Twentieth Century, two celebrated authors investigated these stories separately and subsequently published the results of their spine-chilling experiences at the dilapidated mansion Castel a Mare.

Violet Tweedale (1862-1936) wrote poetry, novels and over thirty books on the occult. A committed spiritualist, she attended séances with many distinguished people including two prime ministers, Arthur Balfour and William Gladstone. In 1912, while wintering in Torquay, she was intrigued by gossip of screams heard coming from the empty house with footsteps of unseen people running along corridors and upon the stairs. Accompanied by her husband, the couple obtained the house keys from the owner, an elderly builder, who gave his permission to investigate the phenomena. The Tweedales made several lunchtime visits and soon became aware that doors were in the habit of locking and unlocking themselves. Violet noted that 'the ghosts laughed to scorn such securities as locks and keys' as carefully secured doors were frequently flung wide open, leaving no trace of footprints on twigs and straw laid on the floor by the intrepid ghost hunters. The author's attention was particularly drawn to the bathroom, which, she intuitively knew was the focal point of the ghostly activity.

During wartime, five years later, Violet formed a party of eight people including a medium and returned to conduct more psychic research at Castel a Mare. The medium entered the bathroom where her being was taken over by the entity of an infuriated man who angrily approached the party shouting obscenities. She was then taken over by a fresh control, a weeping female servant, who gave a piercing scream and grasped her throat as if in the throes of strangulation, 'Terrible Doctor – will kill me – he has killed master – help! help!'. Collapsing unconscious to

Violet Tweedale

the floor, the medium was brought round and confirmed that an insane doctor had killed the master of the house, then strangled a maidservant who had witnessed the murderous attack.

On a Sunday evening, in 1917, the same year that Violet Tweedale took the medium to Castel a Mare, a budding best-selling author, playwright, journalist and composer, Beverley Nichols (1898-1983), who had been educated in Torquay where he lived with his family at Cleave Court, was returning from Evensong with his brother Paul and their friend Lord Peter St Audries. Passing the haunted house, the boys decided to explore the place and three hours later, armed with a crucifix and candles to ward off evil, the teenagers climbed through a window, propping it open with a stick in case they were confronted by a ghost and needed to make a hasty exit. Making a tour of the house they approached the bathroom where Violet Tweedale's medium had encountered supernatural beings. Beverley suddenly felt a black veil engulfing his mind and he staggered down the stairs and fell through the window before lapsing into unconscious-

Beverley Nichols

ness. He quickly recovered and, after checking he was all right, his concerned colleagues bravely re-entered the house but, after a thorough search found nothing untoward. Believing that Paul was a negative influence, Peter then insisted on going back unaccompanied and the young friends kept in communication by whistling reassuringly to each other. Suddenly, the lone ghost hunter shouted, 'Oh, my God', before hurriedly emerging looking as though he had indeed seen the proverbial ghost.

Beverley and Paul quickly took their friend to a neighbour's house and after gulping down some brandy, Peter revealed his terrifying tale:

> I wasn't particularly hopeful of seeing anything. However, something seemed to tell me if there *were* to be any *manifestations*, that is to say, quite crudely, if there was a ghost, the centre of its activity would be in that little room. …I suppose that about twenty minutes must have gone by like this, and I was thinking of giving it up as a bad job. Your last whistle had just sounded, and growing impatient, I began to rise to my feet, intending to have a final look at the little room, and then to go home.
>
> Then, the thing happened. Out of that room, down the darkness of the corridor, something rushed, I don't know what it was, except that it was black, and seemed to be shaped like a man. But two things I did notice. The first was that I could see no face – only blackness. The

> second was that it made no noise. It rushed towards me over the bare floor without a sound. ... After that I was knocked flat on my back by some overwhelming force. I had a sickening, overwhelming sensation of evil, as though I were struggling with something beastly, out of Hell... I remember struggling – it seemed to me for my life- staggering with an incredible effort to my feet – and fighting my way downstairs. ...There was nothing but darkness and a hundred filthy influences sapping my strength. The next thing I remember is meeting you outside.

Naturally, following this unpleasant experience, the boys were keen to discover the dark history of Castel a Mare and paid a visit to a psychic with an international reputation living close by. She listened calmly to their story and then, without recourse to her special powers, she relied on hearsay to give a variation on the explanation given by Violet Tweedale's medium. According to Beverley Nichols' source, there had been a double murder in the house some forty years earlier, when an insane doctor attacked and killed, not his patient, but his wife, before slaying a maidservant who had witnessed the crime in the bathroom. No evidence has been found to verify either of these claims, though since the house was converted into four separate dwellings in the 1920s, no further incidents of supernatural activity have been reported from the site of the mysterious Castel a Mare.

ISADORA DUNCAN & PARIS SINGER

The Lovers of Oldway Mansion

Paris Singer (1868-1932), christened in honour of the city of his birth, inherited millions from the world's leading sewing-machine magnate Isaac Singer and transformed his late American father's beloved Devon villa, dubbed the 'Wigwam', into the magnificent neo-classical Oldway Mansion which became known as Paignton's Versailles. Since its completion in 1907, there have been so many unexplained happenings in the building that at one point members of the local Spiritualist Church were called in to conduct an exorcism. Paris has been recognised as one of the ghosts that are regularly seen peering through windows or walking through solid walls, and there was a solitary appearance by the spirit of his mistress, the visionary innovator of modern dance, Isadora Duncan (1878-1927).

The controversial American dance artiste upset the establishment but entranced audiences across Europe and was a living legend when she began an eight-year affair with Paris Singer in 1909. He supported her extravagant life-style and she tolerated the fact that he was a married man with five children conceding that 'travelling with a millionaire simplifies things'. An advocate of unconventional living and 'free love' that clashed with the moral standards of the day, she flaunted numerous lovers in public and was already the unmarried mother of a daughter when she further scandalised society by giving birth in France to a son fathered by Singer. Isadora and her entourage of child students were immediately transported across the Channel by Singer who accommodated them at Oldway Mansion. Once the dancer had recovered her figure, it was not long before she developed 'itchy feet'. Torn between her need for love and her art, she chose the latter and abandoned the luxurious lifestyle with her lover, whom she recorded, had '14 automobiles in the garage and a yacht in the harbour'.

Whilst touring Russia in 1913, Isadora had a terrifying premonition where she saw the bodies of children lying in coffins. That night she felt compelled to dance to Chopin's *Funeral March*. Her worst fears were realised when Paris told her the dreadful news that her two children had drowned in France. Riding in a car accompanied by their nurse, the vehicle had stalled and when the chauffeur left his seat to crank the engine, he forgot to apply the handbrake allowing the car to lurch forward and plunge into the River Seine. Isadora refused to believe persistent rumours that one of Singer's other mistresses had bribed the driver to commit murder and soon the couple were expecting another child. Sadly, the baby died shortly after being born in August 1914. A few days earlier, World War One had been declared and death became no

Isadora Duncan (from a painting).

stranger at Oldway Mansion, which was utilised as a war hospital for allied troops. The hospital was run by American women, among them Lady Randolph Churchill the mother of future premier Winston Churchill. An honour was bestowed upon the town when Paignton received its first royal visit from a reigning monarch. Queen Mary spoke words of comfort to the wounded during a private visit to Oldway and consented to be photographed on the terrace with Paris and his estranged wife Lily.

The long tempestuous affair between Paris and Isadora ended in 1917 and following the Armistice, Oldway Mansion was used only occasionally by Singer. The split with Isadora failed to revive his marriage and his wife divorced him. At the age of 50, his life was at a crossroads and stating that crippling taxation laws had driven him out of England, he decided to divide his time between his estates in France and America. He was instrumental in developing Palm Beach as a millionaire's playground, before heart trouble brought about his death whilst staying at a London hotel in 1932.

Ten years earlier, Isadora had married a Russian poet and embarked upon a tour of America where she was denounced by the press as 'a Bolshevik hussy' who did not 'wear enough clothes to pad a crutch'. The dancer was rendered destitute and once again it was Paris Singer who provided financial assistance which enabled her to purchase tickets for the voyage back to Europe where her husband left her and committed suicide.

In September 1927, Paignton Urban District Council met to discuss the possibility of approaching Singer with a view to purchasing the property he had vacated at Oldway. On that very same day, Isadora Duncan tragically met her death in Nice. Riding with her latest male companion in his Bugatti open top sports car, the fringes of her long shawl became entangled in the spokes of the rear wheel and she was instantly

Paris Singer (fifth from left) stands alongside his wife and Queen Mary.

garrotted. As rescuers tried in vain to cut away the tightly bound scarf from her broken neck, her suitor stood by her side weeping and crying: 'I've killed the Madonna'. Before the shocking news was broken to the world, a servant girl was cleaning at the foot of the grand staircase at Oldway Mansion, when she was astonished to see the figure of a beautiful bare-footed woman clad in a flimsy Greek chiton, dancing along the balcony at the top of the stairs before disappearing like a 'will o' the wisp'. Perhaps the spirit of Isadora was drawn to her first love – the sea. Raised in San Francisco she wrote: 'I was born by the sea and I have noticed that all the great events of my life have taken place by the sea. My first idea of movement, of the dance, certainly came from the rhythm of the waves. I was born under the star of Aphrodite'. In France, Isadora's friends recalled her last words before her fateful last journey: 'Adieu my friends, I go on to glory!'

LILLIE LANGTRY

The Lady in Blue

The celebrated actress Lillie Langtry (1852-1929) was the darling of society in Victorian London. An attractive, forceful, ambitious lady who was a phenomenon of the age. To men worldwide she was the personification of beauty and everything that was desirable in a woman. Author George Bernard Shaw wryly observed: 'I resent Mrs Langtry, she has no right to be intelligent, daring and independent as well as lovely. It is a frightening combination of attributes'.

Lillie Langtry.

Pear's soap used Lillie's endorsement in their advertisements and her picture was buried at the base of Cleopatra's Needle when it was erected on the Embankment. Millais painted her portrait, Gladstone read Shakespeare to her and Oscar Wilde slept on her doorstep as a token of his adoration. In America the notorious Judge Roy Bean was her most ardent admirer and named the Texas town of Langtry in her honour dispensing justice from his saloon the Jersey Lily. Wooed by royalty, Lillie used the royal patronage and her illicit affair with Edward VII to launch a spectacularly successful theatrical career on both sides of the Atlantic.

Lillie was born in Jersey and christened Emillie Le Breton by her father who was dean of the island. In March 1874, Lillie married Edward Langtry and the newly-weds set sail for a romantic honeymoon aboard the groom's luxury yacht *Red Gauntlet*. After calling into Torquay to visit members of Lillie's family who resided at Braddons Cliffe, the couple lived at sea for a year and the relationship was already strained by the time they returned to the town and took up residence for three months at the villa Engadina.

The marriage foundered when Lillie realised her husband was not wealthy enough to sustain the lifestyle she craved. Moving to London she established herself as a leading socialite and in 1877 became the first royal mistress to be flaunted in public by Edward, the Prince of Wales, known as 'Bertie' to his circle of family and friends and revealingly, 'Dirty Bertie' by his critics. Society gossips had a field day but unabashed by the scandal or its effect on his wife Alexandra, the prince provided a home in Bournemouth for Lillie. Cocking a snook at the critics she cheekily named it The Red House and had the words 'They say – What say they? Let them say?' inscribed in the plasterwork. The ghosts of Edward and Lillie are said to haunt their Bournemouth love nest, which is now the Langtry Manor Hotel, and the presence of their spirits reportedly disrupted the filming of a television series about them.

The relationship 'cooled' in more ways than one when Lillie upset her royal lover by dropping ice down his back at a public function. Bertie was not amused and he turned his attention to another mistress, Daisy 'Babbling' Brooke, the Countess of Warwick. Lillie retaliated by having an affair with Edward's nephew, Prince Louis Battenberg (the father of Lord Louis Mountbatten who was killed by the IRA in 1979). Lillie gave birth to a daughter who grew up to become the mother of Mary Malcolm, one of the first women presenters to appear on BBC Television. Lillie's daughter believed she was the lovechild of Bertie until the day of her wedding when her mother revealed the true identity of her father to be Prince Louis.

The Prince of Wales.

January 1901 signalled the end of the Victorian age when the Queen died after a reign of sixty-four years. Princess Alexandra tolerated her husband's numerous flagrant extra-marital affairs with all the dignity she could muster, but her patience must have been severely tested at the Coronation. For, tactlessly positioned together among the invited VIP's were three of Bertie's most prominent mistresses, Daisy Brook, Alice Keppel and Lillie Langtry. Lillie had married Hugo de Bathe two years earlier following the death by alcoholism of the long-suffering Edward Langtry. It appears that neither this new marriage nor King Edward's accession to the throne did anything to deter a love affair that had spanned three decades. A few months after his mother's death Bertie evidently installed his mistress at Dunstone (now the Warberry Nursing Home) in Torquay and visited her periodically from his yacht anchored in the bay. To the astonishment of local historians who have found no proof to support this story, the legend gained credence in 1974 when the Department of Environment issued a preservation order to save the property from demolition because 'the large stucco villa was originally the summer residence of Lillie Langtry for whom it was purchased by King Edward VII apparently'.

A solicitor acting for the owners said he could only assume that the Department of Environment had access to some secret information, possibly memoirs, that had not been made available to the public. Some years before the villa was registered as a listed building it had been converted into two hotels, Dunstone and Audrey Court. Although the latter had originally been nothing more than the stables and servants quarters of the building, the proprietor told a reporter from the *Herald Express* in 1976, that he once knew an elderly man who claimed to have worked as the gardener's help and boot boy at the villa during Lillie's stay. He also revealed that the ghost of the 'Jersey Lily' walks the corridors of the hotel, apparently still waiting for the day her prince will come. For, a 'lady in blue' had been seen by several guests: 'I have seen her on the stairs' he said. 'The last time I just had a glance at her and then she disappeared. She is a beautiful woman in royal blue Edwardian dress. She seems to have greyish hair and is in her fifties'.

LADY NANCY ASTOR

A Yankee at King Arthur's Court

The unruly behaviour of Members of Parliament in the House of Commons is matched by a ghost, which disrupts them when they escape the pressures of work to imbibe alcohol. In December 1998, a national newspaper reported that staff working in the popular Strangers Bar had seen glasses throwing themselves off shelves and a wine glass moving across the bar unaided by human hand. Perhaps it was no coincidence that this story appeared on the 80th anniversary of the 1918 General Election when women had been first allowed to vote. Before the saloon was built the area had been set aside for lady members and the first woman to enjoy this privilege was Nancy Astor (1879-1964), a zealous teetotaller and tireless advocator of temperance who would doubtless prefer that hers was the only 'spirit' to be allowed in this historic part of the Commons.

Born in Danville, Virginia, Nancy was the daughter of Chiswell Langhorne, a Civil War veteran who had made a fortune in post-war railroad construction. The beautiful, vivacious southern belle was 27 years old with one disastrous marriage behind her when she met wealthy socialite Waldorf

In this satirical cartoon, the ghosts of Robert Walpole, Queen Bess, William Gladstone and Benjamin Disraeli gaze at the picture of Lady Astor in the House of Commons and ask 'But why?'

Astor on board a liner travelling to England. After a whirlwind courtship the couple were wed in 1906. Her friend American cowboy comic Will Rogers later quipped: 'Nancy, you sure out-married yourself'. She had a firm belief in the superiority of the female species and countered: 'I married beneath me – all women do'.

Waldorf had been born in New York on the same day as Nancy. His father Viscount William Astor had not endeared himself to his fellow countrymen when he moved his family to England in 1899 publicly stating: 'America is not a fit place for a gentleman to live'. Becoming a British subject ten years later, he took a short cut to a peerage by becoming a newspaper tycoon.

In 1908, Waldorf entered politics. Refusing the offer of a safe seat, he became the Tory candidate for Plymouth Sutton, attracted by it's historical association with the Pilgrim Fathers and America. Two years later at the second attempt he won the seat from the Liberals. During World War One he served as parliamentary private secretary to Prime Minister, David Lloyd George, before his career in the Commons came to end upon the death of his father in 1919. Waldorf inherited the peerage and was obliged to move to the House of Lords.

The part played by women in British society while men were at war had finally won them the vote and the right to stand for Parliament. Lady Astor became the first successful women candidate when she fought a by-election and won the seat vacated by her husband, which she was to hold for twenty-five years. In her maiden speech she requested: 'I do not want you to look on your lady member as a fanatic or lunatic. I am simply trying to speak for the hundreds of women and children throughout the country who cannot speak for themselves'.

Her plea fell on deaf ears, the 'woman in the house' was mocked relentlessly, her presence bitterly resented in a hitherto exclusive gentleman's club with no facilities for women. Winston Churchill could not bring himself to speak to her in the Commons for years. When Nancy confronted him about his attitude he replied: 'Well, when you entered the House of Commons I felt as though some woman had entered my bathroom and I had nothing to protect myself with except a sponge'.

A controversy ensued when a painting of Nancy's historic entry into Parliament flanked by Lloyd George and Arthur Balfour was removed from the House of Commons following petty protests that it was a dangerous precedent to have a picture portraying living politicians.

Nancy gradually overcame male bias. As a spirited opponent of socialism, a champion of women's rights and children's welfare, she won popularity as one of the most flamboyant personalities in British public life. During World War Two, Waldorf and Nancy were Lord and Lady Mayor of Plymouth and firebombs hit their home Astor House on the Hoe during the first serious raid of the Blitz. Displaying the bulldog spirit of her adopted country Lady Astor donned her tin helmet and went up on the roof to inspect the damage. With glass splinters in her hair from the shattered windows, she shouted: 'Where in the hell are the buckets of sand for the roof?'

When Nancy retired from politics at the end of the war, the Astors had served the people of Plymouth for thirty-five years. Waldorf died in 1952, having supervised the reconstruction plans for the war-ravaged city. On her 80th birthday in 1959, Nancy became the only woman to be honoured with the Freedom of Plymouth. She died on 2 May 1964 after a stroke. Her ashes were buried wrapped in a Confederate flag and it appears she continues to be a 'Rebel' beyond the grave haunting Westminster where she was insultingly dismissed by her critics as a 'Yankee at King Arthur's Court'.

LAWRENCE OF ARABIA

Sons of Thunder

One of the Twentieth Century's most enigmatic heroes, TE Lawrence, (1888-1935) turned down a recommendation for the Victoria Cross and the offer of a knighthood for his role as guerrilla leader of the Arab Revolt against Germany's allies the Turks during the First World War. The 'Uncrowned King of the Desert' was a brilliant scholar, philosopher, archaeologist, linguist, author, diplomat and statesman, who shunned fame and fortune to become an aircraft mechanic, in what was a forlorn attempt to escape the charismatic image he had engendered as the world renowned 'Lawrence of Arabia'.

One of Lawrence's ancestors was the cousin of Sir Walter Raleigh, a connection of which he was extremely proud, therefore, it was fitting that in February 1929, Lawrence journeyed to the county of Raleigh's birth to be stationed at RAF Mountbatten, Plymouth. In an effort to escape undue attention he had assumed the alias 'Shaw', in honour of his great friend, Irish playwright George Bernard Shaw, who introduced him to the vivacious Lady Nancy Astor. She was one of the most glamorous figures of the inter-war period and had the distinction of being the first female to enter Parliament after women had been given their long overdue right to vote in 1918. She succeeded her husband, Waldorf, as member for Plymouth Sutton when he moved to the Lords, and continued to serve the city until she retired from politics in 1945.

Lawrence was asexual and a cynical woman-hater but became an ardent admirer of American-born Nancy and her incredible zest for life. She was the only female allowed to ride pillion on his motorbike. The pair would often shoot off on his powerful 1000cc Brough Superior for a high speed ride around the city and boasted of reaching speeds of 90mph along Plymouth Embankment. In October 1930, Lawrence wrote to tell Nancy how he had overtaken a Bentley sports car 'which only did 88' on Salisbury Plain: 'I wished I had had a peeress or two on my flapper bracket'.

Lawrence called his bike *Boenerges* (meaning Sons of Thunder, the name which Jesus gave to two of his disciples James and John), but his love of speed was to cause his tragic death shortly after his discharge from the RAF in March 1935. Taking up residence at Cloud's Hill, a rented cottage in Dorset, he found it difficult to face an uncertain future and friends became concerned as he had attempted suicide in the past, he wrote to Nancy: 'I am so tired that it feels like heaven drawing near: only there are people who whisper that heaven will bore me. When they tell me that I almost wish I were dead for I have done everything in life except rest, and if rest is to prove no refuge, then what is left?'

Lady Astor tried to cheer Lawrence with the promise of a forthcoming government post and invited him to her country

Lawrence of Arabia.

house in Buckinghamshire: 'I believe… you will be asked to help reorganise the Defence Forces. If you will come to Cliveden, the last Saturday in May… you will never regret it'.

Britain needed men of Lawrence's calibre in preparing to counter the growing threat posed by Germany. On the 13 May, Lawrence received a letter from the award-winning author of *Tarka the Otter*, Henry Williamson, based in Georgeham, North

Devon, proposing a meeting at Cloud's Hill to discuss the possibility of Lawrence holding talks with Adolf Hitler to try and secure a lasting peace in Europe. Williamson was a member of Oswald Mosely's British Union of Fascists and fervent admirer of the Fuerer's achievements. His collected novels *The Flax of Dream* contained the following dedication: 'I salute the great man across the Rhine whose life symbol is a happy child'.

Lawrence agreed to receive Williamson and rode to the Post Office to send a telegram with the following directions: 'Lunch Tuesday will find cottage one mile north of Bovington Camp SHAW'.

On his way back home he swerved to avoid two errand boys on bicycles, crashed and flew over the handlebars, receiving severe head injuries. First on the scene of the accident was the driver of a passing army truck, Ron Morgan, whose family lived in the Dartmoor village of Holne. Lawrence was taken to Bovington Military Hospital, but never recovered consciousness. Nancy did not go to visit Lawrence and seemed to be in a state of denial, refusing to believe that his life was in danger. The truth was brought home to her six days after the accident when the terrible news of his death was announced as she was holding a celebratory lunch with friends to mark the occasion of her birthday, which she shared with her husband who was born on the same day.

Nancy was stricken with grief and remarked how she had ridden with Lawrence only two weeks earlier: 'He liked it because I could balance without touching him'.

The ghost of Lawrence wearing flowing long Arab robes was soon spotted riding a motorbike by Cloud's Hill, and two weeks after Lady Astor's death in May 1964, made an appearance in Plymouth on what would have been Nancy's 85th birthday. Late that night, a local businessman was walking his dog along Plymouth Embankment when he heard a mixture of laughter and the roar of a motorbike. He turned to see it flash by in a blaze of light driven by Lawrence wearing RAF uniform with a youthful, stylishly attired Nancy riding pillion. A personal friend of Lawrence, the astounded onlooker had visited Cloud's Hill a month before his fatal accident and found that Lawrence felt the end was near. The superstitious Lawrence was convinced that he had received an omen of doom when a robin tapped on his bedroom window three mornings in a row. Chillingly, a year before his death, Lawrence had also prophesised his demise in a letter to motorbike manufacturer George Brough: 'It looks as though I might yet break my neck on a Brough Superior'.

JOHN SLATER

The Show Must Go On

Genial cockney actor John Slater (1916-1975) became known to millions of television viewers as Sergeant Stone in the phenomenally successful 1960's BBC crime series 'Z Cars'. He had earlier established himself in show business alongside Brian Rix in the famous 'Whitehall Farces', written and presented a series of story-telling slots on radio and was a familiar figure to cinema audiences appearing in Ealing Studio classics *Always Rains on Sunday, Against the Wind and Passport to Pimlico.* At the height of his fame he underwent heart surgery after collapsing whilst playing in a charity cricket match in 1971. Despite this setback, John returned to the stage the following year and resurrected the fortunes of the Brixham Theatre, where he produced and starred in plays for the next two summer seasons, before his health problems returned and a prolonged illness resulted in his death at the National Heart Hospital, Harefield.

The fact that John Slater had lived long enough to become famous was nothing short of a miracle. In 1946, he had a close brush with death, when he and his wife Betty were two of only four people to survive an air disaster in which twenty-one passengers and crew lost their lives. The couple had married five years earlier in a wartime ceremony and were returning from a long delayed honeymoon in Paris, when the Dakota aeroplane in which they were travelling crash-landed. John was thrown clear through the fuselage and was seriously injured but went back to rescue his trapped wife who was badly burned. They had another narrow escape when two fuel tanks exploded whilst they were crawling out of the wreckage. Not surprisingly, this harrowing experience served to stimulate an interest in the afterlife and during John's first season at the Shakespeare Memorial Theatre in Stratford-on-Avon, the Slaters became aware of the ghost of a 'lady in blue' whilst staying at the house where the Bard's daughter had once lived.

John Slater.

Betty Slater presented a bust of her late husband as a memorial to the Brixham Theatre. On that very day, members of staff became aware of a ghostly presence. In the morning, the theatre manageress caught a glimpse of a man walking along the passageway towards the locked hospitality rooms reserved for performers and their guests, but when she immediately followed him to investigate, there was no one to be seen and no other exit from which he could have avoided her. After the evening show, the box office lady was preparing to go home and was preoccupied buttoning up her coat when someone approached. She thoughtfully moved her basket to one side to give a gentleman room to pass, but when she looked up to see who it was, the corridor was empty. The next day, when the two ladies related the strange incidents to each other, it became apparent that the person they had seen had been wearing pin striped trousers, grey gaiters and black shoes – the costume that John Slater had worn during his first production at the theatre called *Wanted One Body*.

John Slater's tenure of the theatre, in the town where he had bought a home in 1964, had been threatened by a reluctant warning to owners Torbay Council that he might not present another show there if they continued to ignore his requests to carry out improvements and give the theatre a new look. However, even beyond the grave it became apparent to technicians that John still had 'hands on' control of productions in the theatre he had proudly restored to success. Stage lights would mysteriously light up when the theatre was empty and orchestra cue lights were often found on in the morning after being carefully switched off after a performance the night before. The back stage stairs became a 'no-go' area for usherettes who sensed an eerie presence and avoided venturing there alone as they felt they were being 'followed'. In 1987, an electrician set up the sound mixer and lighting board for the opening performance of the summer show, but when he returned the next day, the settings had somehow been altered overnight to resemble the sequence favoured by John Slater during his initial production in 1972.

On hearing of the respected artiste's death, Shaun Sutton, head of BBC Television drama paid this tribute to his memory: 'John Slater was an actor of high talent and a man of personal courage. For the last years of his life he suffered considerable heart trouble, but he refused to let this interfere with his work. He remained active almost to the end. His professional life was extraordinarily full covering hundreds of films, television and stage plays. He will be missed by thousands of friends throughout the theatrical world'. This statement was undeniably true. Equally, there is little doubt amongst the people who knew and worked with him during his happy spell at Brixham Theatre, that the spirit of John Slater also missed them and continued to be drawn by the 'smell of the greasepaint and the roar of the crowd!' He was also an extremely superstitious person who stood by the acting fraternity's traditional belief that whenever adversity strikes 'the show must go on!'

UNCLE TOM COBLEY & ALL

The Grey Mare of Widecombe Fair

In Los Angeles there is an exclusive 'charity shop' where famous people donate personal possessions to be sold for worthy causes. Among the fabulous gowns once worn by Elizabeth Taylor and the gold discs awarded to Cher, there was a piece of Devonshire pottery that immediately caught my eye during a visit in the mid-1990s. Previously owned by Barbara Striesand it was a drinking mug featuring the legendary figures of 'Old Uncle Tom Cobley and all' sitting astride Tom Pearce's grey mare. How this item of bric-a-brac came to be in the possession of a singing superstar is a mystery, although it confirms the international appeal of Devon's best known folksong 'Widecombe Fair'.

The humorous, yet poignant tale tells the simple story of a journey undertaken by seven men on a borrowed steed which collapses and dies while trying to carry them all home after a day of merriment and wassailing at the fair. As a result, the mare and her passengers are doomed to roam Eternity and can be seen 'when the wind whistles cold on the moor at night'. The tune was first collected and published by the Reverend

Uncle Tom Cobley: an early re-enactment at Widecombe.

Sabine Baring-Gould in 1890 and contains the well-worn chorus featuring the familiar cast of characters: 'For I want for to go to Widecombe Fair, With Bill Brewer, Jan Stewer, Peter Gurney, Peter Davy, Dan'l Whiddon, Harry Hawke, Old Uncle Tom Cobley and all'. Little wonder that when the event Devon Sings – a simultaneous sing-along held in towns and cities to raise money for the charity Children in Need – was held in September 2008, crowds and choirs across Devon gathered to perform the county's most celebrated ghost story.

Whether Tom Cobley, or the other characters ever actually existed has been the subject of much debate, although, the inhabitants of Spreyton certainly believe so. The village has made the most of its link with the folksong and boasts a Tom Cobley Cottage and a Tom Cobley Tavern. Research by the

Widecombe and District Local History Group suggests that the grey mare's passengers were real people who left Spreyton and made the twelve-mile journey to a livestock market at Widecombe in 1802. The name Tom Cobley was a popular one in the Spreyton area, although the one most likely referred to in the song has been identified from a grave in the local churchyard where 82 years-old Thomas Cobley was buried in 1844. However, killjoys have cast doubt on this theory, since they argue that the earliest recorded annual fair at Widecombe was held in 1850. Despite this carping criticism, most people are content to believe the lament of the unnamed narrator – seemingly the nephew of Old Uncle Tom Cobley:

Widecombe-in-the-Moor.

Tom Pearce, Tom Pearce, lend me your grey mare.
All along, down along, out along lee.
For I want for to go to Widecombe Fair,
With Bill Brewer, Jan Stewer, Peter Gurney,
Peter Davy, Dan'l Whiddon, Harry Hawke,
Old Uncle Tom Cobley and all,
Old Uncle Tom Cobley and all.

And when shall I see again my grey mare?
All along, down along, out along lee.
By Friday soon, or Saturday noon,
With Bill Brewer, Jan Stewer, Peter Gurney,
Peter Davy, Dan'l Whiddon, Harry Hawke,
Old Uncle Tom Cobley and all,
Old Uncle Tom Cobley and all.

So they harnessed and bridled the old grey mare.
All along, down along, out along lee.
And off they drove to Widecombe Fair,
With Bill Brewer, Jan Stewer, Peter Gurney,
Peter Davy, Dan'l Whiddon, Harry Hawke,
Old Uncle Tom Cobley and all,
Old Uncle Tom Cobley and all.

Then Friday came, and Saturday noon.
All along, down along, out along lee.
But Tom Pearce's old mare hath not trotted home,
With Bill Brewer, Jan Stewer, Peter Gurney,
Peter Davy, Dan'l Whiddon, Harry Hawke,
Old Uncle Tom Cobley and all,
Old Uncle Tom Cobley and all.

So Tom Pearce he got up to the top o' the hill.
All along, down along, out along lee.
And he see'd his old mare down a-making her will,
With Bill Brewer, Jan Stewer, Peter Gurney,
Peter Davy, Dan'l Whiddon, Harry Hawke,
Old Uncle Tom Cobley and all,
Old Uncle Tom Cobley and all.

So Tom Pearce's old mare, her took sick and died.
All along, down along, out along lee.
And Tom he sat down on a stone, and he cried
With Bill Brewer, Jan Stewer, Peter Gurney,
Peter Davy, Dan'l Whiddon, Harry Hawke,
Old Uncle Tom Cobley and all,
Old Uncle Tom Cobley and all.

But this isn't the end o' this shocking affair.
All along, down along, out along lee.
Nor, though they be dead, of the horrid career
Of Bill Brewer, Jan Stewer, Peter Gurney,
Peter Davy, Dan'l Whiddon, Harry Hawke,
Old Uncle Tom Cobley and all,
Old Uncle Tom Cobley and all.

When the wind whistles cold on the moor of a night.
All along, down along, out along lee.
Tom Pearce's old mare doth appear ghastly white,
With Bill Brewer, Jan Stewer, Peter Gurney,
Peter Davy, Dan'l Whiddon, Harry Hawke,
Old Uncle Tom Cobley and all,
Old Uncle Tom Cobley and all.

And all the long night be heard skirling and groans.
All along, down along, out along lee.
From Tom Pearce's old mare in her rattling bones,
With Bill Brewer, Jan Stewer, Peter Gurney,
Peter Davy, Dan'l Whiddon, Harry Hawke,
Old Uncle Tom Cobley and all,
Old Uncle Tom Cobley and all.

BIBLIOGRAPHY

Coleman, Stanley Jackson. Lore of Devon, Isle of Man, Folklore Academy, 1955

Devon Folklife Register. Shades and Spectres: A Guide to Devon Hauntings. Exeter 1978

Hippesley Coxe, A.D. Haunted Britain, London, Hutchinson, 1973

Holgate, Mike. Along the River Dart, Stroud, Tempus Publishing, 1999

Holgate, Mike. Murder & Crime: Devon, Stroud, Tempus Publishing, 2007

Kipling, Rudyard. Something of Myself, London, Macmillan & Co., 1937

Matthews, H.C.G. and Harris, Brian (eds) Oxford Dictionary of National Biography, Oxford, Oxford University Press, 2004

Morgan, Eileen. Beatrice Chase of Widecombe, Teignmouth, Brunswick Press Ltd., 1974

Nichols, Beverley. Twenty-Five, London, Jonathan Cape, 1926

Prince, John. Worthies of Devon, London, Longman, 1810

Turner, James Ernest. Ghosts in the Southwest, Newton Abbot, David & Charles, 1973

Tweedale, Violet. Ghosts I Have Seen, London, Herbert Jenkins Ltd., 1919

Widecombe and District Local History Group. The History of Widecombe Fair, Chudleigh, Orchard Publications, 2007

Journals and Periodicals:

Dartmouth Chronicle, Devon Life, Express & Echo, Herald Express, Mid Devon Advertiser, News of the World, South Hams Times, The Times, Totnes Times, Western Morning News, Western Times